LETTERS OF NOT

Dale Shaw

The Friday Project
An imprint of HarperCollinsPublishers
77–85 Fulham Palace Road
Hammersmith, London W6 8JB
www.harpercollins.co.uk

First published by The Friday Project in 2014

1

A catalogue record for this book
is available from the British Library

ISBN 978-0-00-753310-7

Text and image design by We Are Laura

Other image copyright information:
From Getty Images, photographs by: Charles Gullung, Will Steacy,
Tom Roberton, SuperStock, Siede Preis
From Shutterstock, photographs by: Kamira, Annykos,
Vereshchagin Dmitry, David M. Schrader, GoDog Photo, Burnell

Printed and bound in China

Find out more about HarperCollins and the environment at
www.harpercollins.co.uk/green

For Lucy,

Obviously x

CONTENTS

00 INTRODUCTION 08

01 DR HEIMLICH'S NOTE TO A COLLEAGUE 13

02 WERNER HERZOG'S NOTE TO HIS CLEANING LADY 14

03 LANCE ARMSTRONG WRITES TO A FAN 18

04 POPE BENEDICT XVI's HANDOVER NOTES 20

05 WILLIAM BURROUGHS REWRITES THE SWIMMING POOL RULES 25

06 A MODEL WRITES TO AUGUSTE RODIN 28

07 LOU REED WRITES TO A TELEVISION PRODUCER 30

08 JAMES JOYCE'S OUT OF OFFICE 34

09 ORSON WELLES' SUGGESTIONS FOR TRANSFORMERS: THE MOVIE 36

10 A LETTER FROM A WISE MAN 39

11 A DOCTOR WRITES TO LOU GEHRIG 42

12 TWEETS FROM THE 1965 NEWPORT FOLK FESTIVAL 44

13 A NOTE FROM ALEXANDER GRAHAM BELL'S BUSINESS MANAGER 50

14 A PUBLISHER WRITES TO GEOFFREY CHAUCER 52

15 BRIAN ENO'S DISCARDED OBLIQUE STRATEGIES   55

16 A CHRISTMAS ROUND-ROBIN FROM THE FREUD FAMILY   62

17 TIM BERNERS-LEE'S WORLD WIDE WEB DEVELOPMENT DIARY   65

18 THE HEAD OF THE AMERICAN LIZARD LOVERS   68
    ASSOCIATION WRITES TO JIM MORRISON

19 ALBERT EINSTEIN CONTACTS A PHOTOGRAPHER   70

20 BRIAN JONES' HOPES FOR THE ROLLING STONES   72

21 A POTENTIAL COMPETITION WINNER WRITES TO   78
    ALFRED HITCHCOCK

22 NEIL ARMSTRONG'S LETTER HOME   83

23 LETTER FROM THE TABLE NEXT TO THE   86
    ALGONQUIN ROUND TABLE

24 INFORMATION TO ALL PIZZA ARCHIPELAGO   88
    EMPLOYEES ON THE ARRIVAL OF VAN MORRISON

25 CORMAC McCARTHY GIVES DIRECTIONS   92

26 WILBUR WRIGHT WRITES TO HIS BROTHER   95

27 DAVID SIMON WRITES TO HBO INC   96

28 CHARLES DARWIN WRITES TO HIS AMERICAN PUBLISHER   98

29 ANTI CALIGULA CAMPAIGN AD   102

30 THE MARK E. SMITH AUDIO GUIDE TO RIPON CATHEDRAL   106

31 JANE AUSTEN WRITES TO A LOVE RIVAL   108

32 CAPTAIN SCOTT'S *OTHER* LAST LETTER TO HIS WIFE   112

33 AN EVICTION NOTICE FROM ST FRANCIS
      OF ASSISI'S LANDLORD   116

34 PATTI SMITH'S GYM APPLICATION   118

35 SALVADOR DALI'S TO DO LIST   122

36 A BENEFACTOR CONTACTS BADEN POWELL   125

37 ART GARFUNKEL WRITES TO VAMPIRE WEEKEND   128

38 JOAN OF ARC'S NOTE TO HER CAPTORS   132

39 NOTES FOR BILL GATES' FIRST HIGH SCHOOL REUNION, 1978   136

40 EDGAR ALLAN POE VS. THE BALTIMORE
      SANITATION DEPTARTMENT   140

41 A LOVER REPLIES TO VINCENT VAN GOGH   145

42 BIDDY BAXTER WRITES TO A VIEWER   148

43 NEIL YOUNG'S SHOPPING LIST   150

44 AGATHA CHRISTIE'S JURY DUTY NOTES   154

45 GALILEO GETS A REPLY   158

46 GANDHI WRITES TO HIS DRY CLEANER   163

47 BO DIDDLEY WRITES TO HIS PUBLICIST   170

48 IVAN PAVLOV CONTACTS HIS LOCAL PET STORE   174

49 A LETTER FROM GEORGE ORWELL'S PUBLISHER   176

50 HAROLD PINTER MOVES INTO GREETING CARDS   180

51 BEATRIX POTTER TRIES TO GET AN   184
    OVERDRAFT EXTENSION

    AKNOWLEDGEMENTS   188
    WE ARE LAURA   190

April 2014

My friends,

I can't quite remember why I decided to write a note purportedly from cult German film director Werner Herzog to his fictional cleaning lady. I know where I was: in the kitchen of my flat in Walthamstow, which I was eventually driven out of by an upstairs neighbour with an insatiable love of Speed Garage and lengthy *Call of Duty* sessions ... but that's another introduction entirely.

Being able to correctly identify the inspiration and mechanics involved in the moment of that letter's construction would have come in handy when I had to write a book full of similar material (spoiler alert: It's this book). But anyway, I couldn't. Though the moment definitely happened, because I wrote the letter, had it rejected by someone, felt a bit sad, then wisely sent it to Sabotage Times, where it quickly 'went viral', as I believe the young people say. I had no idea people are as enamoured of Herzog as I am, but it seems the masses can't get enough of that crazy Bavarian and his delightful antics. What baffled me most was the volume of readers who thought it was actually written by him. Even though, as Herzog himself pointed out in an interview, it had my name right next to it.

It seemed sensible to try again, so I went on to write ludicrous missives from other figures I have a healthy obsession with, including Mark E. Smith, Brian Eno, George Orwell, Neil Young and more Brian Eno (I love Brian Eno). Soon, I had unwittingly developed into, as writer Joel Morris put it, 'the BBC4 version of Mike Yarwood'.

However, though a number of these collected letters have been seen before, circulating around the darker reaches of the internet, most are shiny and new. A few didn't make the cut due to legal issues or for reasons of baffling obscurity. You can find some of these at lettersofnot.com, where you can also send your complaints and gift baskets.

A hearty thanks to everyone included in the book who decided not to sue me. You are good eggs. To the others – see you in court.

Dale Shaw
P.S. Full disclosure – I was listening to *Ram* by Paul McCartney as I wrote this.

~~Dear Billy Joel,~~

~~Just who the hell do you think you are, huh? with your big car and your friends?~~

Introduction   April 2014

My friends,

I can't remember why I decided to write a note purportedly from cult German film director Werner Herzog to his fictional cleaning lady. I know where I was: in the kitchen of my flat in Walthamstow which I was eventually driven out of by an upstairs neighbour with an insatiable love of Speed Garage and lengthy Call of Duty sessions... but that's another introduction entirely.

Being able to correctly identify the inspiration and mechanics involved in the moment of that letter's construction would have come in handy when I had to write a book full of similar material. (Spoil

alert: It's this book) But anyway, I couldn't.
Though the moment definitely happened because
I wrote the letter, had it rejected by someone, felt
a bit sad, then wisely sent it to Sabotage Times,
where it quickly 'went viral' as I believe
the young people say. I had no idea people
were as enamoured of Herzog as I am,
but it seems the masses can't get enough
of that crazy Bavarian and his delightful antics.
What baffled me most was the volume of
people who thought it was actually written
by him. Even though, as Herzog himself pointed
out in an interview. It had my name right
next to it.

It seemed sensible to try again, so I
____ to write ludicrous missives from
____ I have a healthy obsession with
including Mark E. Smith, Brian Eno, George Orwell,
Neil Young and more Brian Eno (I love Brian Eno). Soon
I had unwittingly developed into, as writer
Joel Morris put it, 'the BBC4 version of Mike
Yarwood'.

However, though a number of these collected
letters have been seen before, circulating around the
darker reaches of the internet, most are shiny and new.
A few didn't make the cut due to legal
issues or for reasons of baffling obscurity. You
can find some of these at lettersofnot.com
where you can also send your complaints and gift
baskets. A hearty thanks to everyone included in the book who
decided not to sue me. You are good eggs. To
the others — SEE YOU IN COURT. Dale Shaw

P.S. Full disclosure
– I was listening
to 'Ram' by
Paul McCartney
as I wrote this.

Howard,

I've had a great new idea for another
manoeuvre. This one can be used to
pick up women. Pop by the office and
I'll show you how it works.

Henry

Rosalina. Woman.

You constantly revile me with your singular lack of vision. Be aware, there is an essential truth and beauty in all things. From the death throes of a speared gazelle to the damaged smile of a freeway homeless. But that does not mean that the invisibility of something implies its lack of being. Though simpleton babies foolishly believe the person before them vanishes when they cover their eyes during a hateful game of peek-a-boo, this is a fallacy. And so it is that the unseen dusty build up that accumulates behind the DVD shelves in the rumpus room exists also. This is unacceptable.

I will tell you this, Rosalina, not as a taunt or a threat but as an evocation of joy. The joy of nothingness, the joy of the real. I want you to be real in everything you do. If you cannot be real, then a semblance of reality must be maintained. A real semblance of the fake real, or 'real'. I have conquered volcanoes and visited the bitter depths of the earth's oceans. Nothing I have witnessed, from lava to crustacean, assailed me liked the caked debris haunting that small plastic soap hammock in the smaller of the bathrooms. Nausea is not a sufficient word. In this regard, you are not being real.

Now we must turn to the horrors of nature. I am afraid this is inevitable. Nature is not something to be coddled and accepted and held to your bosom like a wounded snake. Tell me, what was there before you were born? What do you remember? That is nature. Nature is a void. An emptiness. A vacuum. And speaking of vacuum, I am not sure you're using the retractable nozzle correctly or applying the 'full weft' setting when attending to the lush carpets of the den. I found some dander there.

15

Reader... When...

you carefully revise me into your original... of war. By another, there is an essential truth.
beauty in all this... from the dear bones of a
special species... to the damaged milk... a
shrewd design. But that does not mean that
the inviolability of something violates it. Each
of them... Though simpletons babies probably
believe the person vanishes when
they cover their eyes during a hateful game
of peek-a-boo. This is a fallacy that do it
about the unseen dust build up... that
accumulates behind the DVD shelves in
the family room every... This is unacceptable
I will tell you this, honour, not as a team, of
a threat... but as an event... so it
realizes this joy of the real felling... it the
real... this joy... do. If you cannot be there,
then... simulacra of reality must be maintained.
A real semblance of the same... or "real"
have captured... volcanoes and mystical... the bitter
depths of the earth's oceans. Nothing... dares
intrepid... from lava to crustacean... avail
me... the caked debris haunting that
small plastic... hammock in the
smaller... the bathrooms. Nausea is not a
sufficient word. In this regard, you are
not big... real.

Now we must turn to the horrors of
nature. I'm afraid this is inevitable.
Nature is not something to be called and
accepted and held to your bosom like
a wounded snake. Tell me what was
there before you were born? What do you
remember? That is nature. Nature is... foul.
An emptiness. A vacuum. And speaking of
vacuums I am not sure you're using the
retractable nozzle correctly, or applying
the "full" wafts setting when attending
to the plush carpets of the den. I sense some
dander there I have... listened to the
Wagner... that I played compulsively from
the eyes of 19 to 24 at least 60 times
a day until the local townsfolk bore
into my dwelling... midnight... pitchfork
and blazing torches. The idea was bad...
appalled me to the point of... emblazon
early grave was like a brick... agony... out.
Music is futile and malicious. So if you
refuse entertain it... reading real...
from the poop radio I was affronted both
recently. Messy... recommend the rec013...
sharp verse... by Goethe. Or Schiller of... you
Sketch... western... If a push...
the situation needs... the spring... again indeed
for I... you will kill it... that is... to... up again
... get the... important... one... are not
... still... before... steel... the fat...
and were... gates of... getting were... smiled
I've been... but now is under the guillotine. Mercy.

I have only listened to two songs in my entire life. One was an aria by Wagner that I played compulsively from the ages of 19 to 27 at least 60 times a day until the local townsfolk drove me from my dwelling using rudimentary pitchforks and blazing torches. The other was Dido. Both appalled me to the point of paralysis. Every quaver was like a brickbat against my soul. Music is futile and malicious. So please, if you require entertainment while organizing the recycling, refrain from the 'pop radio' I was affronted by recently. May I recommend the recitation of some sharp verse. Perhaps by Goethe. Or Schiller. Or Shel Silverstein at a push.

The situation regarding spoons remains unchanged. If I see one, I will kill it.

That is all. Do not fail to think that you are not the finest woman I have ever met. You are. And I am including on this list my mother and the wife of Brad Dourif (the second wife, not the one with the lip thing). Thank you for listening and sorry if parts of this note were smudged. I have been weeping.

Your money is under the guillotine.

Herzog.

25th July 1999

Dear CINDY,

WOW, I mean THANKS SO MUCH for your letter. It just got me so JAZZED!!!!!

I mean, just, God it was AWESOME, so so AWESOME and YES! I do get tired sometimes after a race, but then it makes me feel so ALIVE you know? Do you? YOU KNOW? I just feel GREAT! I've never felt so GREAT!!

But thank you for asking me that and THANK YOU SO MUCH for the gift. I LOVED the texture of it so much and the way it felt against my skin that I may HAVE slightly DESTROYED it by stroking it so hard and SO MUCH. I stroked it to pieces. But I still LOVE IT! Even in PIECES!! PIECES!!

Cindy, I mean, like YES!!! You are the BEST!!! I could just cycle from here in Colorado over to you in New Jersey RIGHT NOW! Because I am so JAZZED that you wrote to me.

Oh man, you hear that? Oh man, I feel a bit weird. OK, I better go outside CINDY!! You RULES!!!!!!!!!!!!!

Lance (JAZZED)

Dear CINDY,

WOW, I mean THANKS SO MUCH! your letter. It just got me so JAZZED I mean, just, God it was AWESOME, AWESOME and YES! I do get tired sometimes after a race, but then makes me feel so ALIVE you know? Do You? YOU KNOW? I just feel GREAT! I've never felt so GRE

But thank you for asking me that on THANK YOU SO MUCH for the gift. I L texture so much and the way it felt a skin that I may HAVE slightly DESTRO it by stroking it so hard and so MUCH! to pieces. But I still LOVE IT! Evenin

Cindy, I mean, like YES!! You are the I could just cycle from here in Color in New Jersey RIGHT NOW! Because so JAZZED that you wrote me. oh man, you hear that? Oh man, I weird. OK, I better g CINDY!! Your

---

To his Divine Holiness the Bishop of Rome, Vicar of Jesus Christ, Successor of the Prince of the Apostles, Supreme Pontiff of the Universal Church, Primate of Italy, Archbishop and Metropolitan of the Roman Province, Sovereign of the Vatican City State, Servant of the servants of God.

Francis,

Buddy, I hope you like shitstorms – because your life just became one.

OK, the van's about to come and pick up my stuff, so I'm jotting this down quickly ...

Get your order in now for some new vestments. Not tomorrow, NOW. I'd expected some fresh ones to be waiting for me when I started, but all I found was an empty closet. And that stuff takes ages to get made up. I've left you a couple of spares in the closet by the vestibule. You're way skinnier than me (you know you are!) but they'll do in a pinch.

The cleaner comes on Thursday mornings and you do not want to be there when she comes. She always wants something blessed. There seems to be a never-ending amount of paraphernalia. She tried to get me to bless one of those mini Pac-Man games; you know, the hand-held ones, for her grandson. I was like, 'I can bless that thing all day, but it's still lame. Unless he's been in a coma since 1989.' I didn't actually say it, but y'know. You'll get stuck with her all morning if you don't run off and hide somewhere.

The window you have to wave out of is in the little study bit. You might know that already but no one told me. First Sunday I was wandering around like Our Saviour in the Wilderness trying to find it. And the Cardinals aren't a bit of use. Great at ring kissing, lousy at directions.

Nuns. Get used to them. They are everywhere, all the time. If you need some 'alone time' lock the door. They have special powers or something and just appear when you least expect it. And they don't say anything, they just stare at you. It's creepy.

To his Divine Holiness the Bishop of Rome, Vicar of Jesus Christ,

Successor of the Prince of the Apostles, Supreme Pontiff of the Universal Church,

Primate of Italy, Archbishop and Metropolitan of the Roman Province,

Sovereign of the Vatican City State,

Servant of the servants of God.

Francis,

Buddy, I hope you like shitstorms — because your life just became one.

OK, the van's about to come and pick up my stuff, so I'm jotting this down quickly ...

Get your order in now for some new vestments. Not tomorrow, NOW. I'd expected some fresh ones to be waiting for me when I started, but all I found was an empty closet. And that stuff takes ages to get made up. I've left you a couple of spares in the closet by the vestibule. You're way skinnier than me (you know you are!) but they'll do in a pinch. The cleaner comes on Thursday mornings and you do not want to be there when she comes. She always wants something blessed. There seems to be a never-ending amount of paraphernalia. She tried to get me to bless one of those mini Pac-Man games; you know, the hand-held ones, for her grandson. I was like, 'I can bless that thing all day, but it's still lame. Unless he's been in a coma since 1989.' I didn't actually say it, but y'know. You'll get stuck with her all morning if you don't run off and hide somewhere.

The window you have to wave out of is in the little study bit. You might know that already but no one told me. First Sunday I was wandering around like Our Savior in the Wilderness trying to find it. And the Cardinals aren't a bit of use. Great at ring kissing, lousy at directions.

Nuns. Get used to them. They are everywhere, all the time. If you need some 'alone time' lock the door. They have special powers or something and just appear when you least expect it. And they don't say anything. they just stare at you. It's creepy.

You're going to be asked a lot of questions about Dan Brown. Do yourself a favour, read The Da Vinci Code. I know, I know, you thought your trials were over and now you'd be on easy street. But honestly, every state function, visit overseas and post-Mass warm down there will be endless theories about it. People think they're being cute asking you about it. They are not. And you'll have to watch the movie too. I'm afraid. It's different. You can probably skip Angels and Demons. You can thank me later. The password for the PC in the office is BONO__101. Don't ask me why, it was that when I arrived. The IT department might have changed it, in which case

You're going to be asked a lot of questions about Dan Brown. Do yourself a favour, read *The Da Vinci Code*. I know, I know, you thought your trials were over and now you'd be on easy street. But honestly, every state function, visit overseas and post-Mass warm down there will be endless theories about it. People think they're being cute asking you about it. They are not. And you'll have to watch the movie too I'm afraid. It's different. You can probably skip *Angels and Demons*. You can thank me later.

The password for the PC in the office is BONO_101. Don't ask me why, it was that when I arrived. The IT department might have changed it, in which case good luck. It's easier changing water into wine than getting an answer from those guys. You need vouchers to use the canteen; I left a few in the desk drawer. God knows why they still use that system. I tried to get it changed – you'd think I was converting to Judaism! The uproar! So anyway, it sucks, but there you are.

Think that's it. No idea where the keys to the Popemobile are. I never knew and no one would tell me. HR should be in touch about your pass. Though they've probably sent you an email about it, which you can't access without your pass, as I found out to my cost. And they tell you that you can't take your picture again if the first one is terrible, but you can, I promise you.

OK, have a blast! Drop me a line when you're settled.

Benedict

P.S. A few people will probably ask if you shit in the woods as well. Just ignore them.

good luck. It's easier changing water into wine than getting an answer from those

guys. You need vouchers to use the canteen, I left a few in the desk drawer. God knows

why they still use that system. I tried to get it changed — you'd think I was converting

Judaism! The uproar! So anyway, it sucks, but there you are.

Think that's it. No idea where the keys to the Popemobile are. I never knew and no

one would tell me. HR should be in touch about your pass. Though they've probably

sent you an email about it, which you can't access without your pass, as I found out to

my cost. And they tell you that you can't take your picture again if the first one is

terrible, but you can. I promise you.

OK, have a blast! Drop me a line when you're settled

Benedict

P.S. A few people will probably ask if you shit in the woods as well.

Just ignore them.

24

No Running – Unless it's shit running down good wholesome American legs, forming oily pools of thunder down amongst dark gray tunnels of hopeless, stubborn rectitude.

No Pushing – Because no one likes the pusherman, firing beautiful dreams into dead undersea veins, charred inside like the mind of his degraded and decadent client. His gray, invisible specter that infects his pleasure on the dullest and the damned.

No Acrobatics or Gymnastics – Or the stacking of young malleable flesh on flesh, building a queer ladder to the stars, leading to my waking life, where I sit totally alone.

No Shouting – You never want to attract the attention of the Controller, lest he lets the drip-drip of technological assassination, decontrolling him or herself from some unspecified central point that haunts the horizon like some blood blister left too long to rot.

No Ducking – Certainly not ducking the empty smell of many years, tied into the deviance that can only come through boredom and the parasitic craving that must be fed though a paranoiac insanity of hopelessness.

No Petting – No vetting, no fretting, no bedwetting. Cut off all biological necessity, it will only make you hard and unsound. Sadistic faces beaten with spiritual famine, hell bouncing off the walls, sickness welcomed like a damaged organism.

WILL PATRONS
KINDLY REFRAIN
FROM

RUNNING

ACROBATICS

GYMNASTICS

SHOOTING

BUCKING

PETTING

THANK YOU!

No Bombing – We need to suffer to show that we are alive and feel that needless, dead-eyed pollution that atrophies and seals off the seductions of the skull.

No Swimming in the Diving Area – Hanging off the board with our ghost fingers, the pink blood filters releasing the odor below you, waiting for you to drop. Above you your enemies circle, waiting to control, like a stuffed animal with glazed eyes bearing down from the wall of a gentleman's club. Below a pool of savage, distended insects all with the face of a burnt nun.

No Smoking – You enter the Smoke Shop and then you see them. Princes of the spirit, arbiters of pang, bureaucrats who equivocate the past, judges who pass sentence on your future, Gods of Zogoth with fiery temples and split, bitter eyes, doctors turning disease into customary abuse, sick children playing with the larvae at their feet, scientists infecting that larvae, the shrill crone beating you for the rent, the bland, majestic soothsayers tearing up your dreams of death and the stiff, sharp seductress squatting over you with their jutting bones and insect ecstasy. Trunk rental available at the snack bar.

12th July 1889

Dear Monsieur Rodin,

 This is the lady who recently posed at your studio for your sculpture 'The Kiss'. Do you happen to have the name of the other model that posed with me? I have some sort of blister that has appeared on my upper lip and I think I may need to get in touch with him.

 Warmest regards,
Sophia

12th July 1889

Dear Monsieur Rodin

       This is the lady who recently
posed at your sculpture 'the kiss'. Do you
happen to know the name of the
other model that posed with me?
I have some sort of blister that
has appeared on my upper lip
and I think I may need to get
in touch with him.

Warmest regards,

Sophia

8th March 1975

Hey Barry, Barry.

Great meeting you at Andy's the other week. You said if I had any ideas for the TV I should drop you a line. Well, I was just sitting here at Max's Kansas City with some friends and we came up with a dynamite idea for a show. Sorry for writing this on bar napkins, wanted to get this down while it was still fresh in my head.

So, here's the idea – BLADIAC!

I play a hard-bitten New York Cop in a leather jacket called Lou Bladiac who investigates New Wave crimes in the music industry. Bladiac don't take no shit and plays by his own rules, while also playing some sweet guitar licks.

You know I did 'Walk on the Wild Side'? So I know quite a bit about the noir stuff and the dark side of life. Well, imagine that song in a TV cop show format. And get this, at the end of each show Bladiac can sing a song about the investigation (which I'll write and perform). Something like 'It was the drummer who did it / he just went ahead and did it …' You see, I just came up with that off the cuff. Imagine how great it would be if I'd put some thought into it. Wait … what … what? Hold on Barry, someone's shouting at me … what? Yeah, I said about the song …

Sorry Barry, so yeah. And Bladiac is handy with a blade, hence his name. That's his main weapon in fighting crime, he uses a switchblade. He don't kill people, just stabs them up a bit before arresting them.

What? Hold on, Rachel's yelling something. No, we said we weren't having the Indian Spirit Guide. No! That's dumb. Oh great, now he/she's crying …

Forget all that Barry, so yeah Bladiac goes undercover and gets in with all these New Wave groups who are doing crimes or are having crimes done against them. He uses disguises and he's a real one for the ladies. And the dudes. He has a female alter ego called Shofanna who's completely convincing. And he has a real great car. And I mentioned the knife thing, right?

31

8th March 1995

Hey Barry, Barry.

Great meeting you at Andy's
the other week you know
if I had any sense on the
TV line. Well, I was
so sort setting down your
at Andy's Kusan City some

...

God, sure there was more to this than that. Lemme think. Bladiac. Cop. New Wave. Blade. Shofanna. Car. Song at the end. Yeah, guess that's it.

Oh wait, guest stars! Yeah, we can get tons of guest stars and people to be in it. I can ask Andy, he loves TV. Maybe he can be the police chief or something. That would be pretty funny. Bowie can be like a snitch. No wait, Iggy can be like a snitch, maybe Bowie can be like a jewel thief or something. Then I, like, stab him up and arrest him.

What did you say? I'll just have a gimlet. Yeah a gin one, they're always gin. Shit, stop distracting me, I keep writing this shit down. Sorry Barry. People keep distracting me. I look really good as a cop. I've got shades and leather jackets, so we can save money on that. And I'm good at playing the tough guy (and the opposite in Shofanna's case). Think this will be a total blast. Put a record out at the end of every season with all the songs I've sung about investigations. Bladiac! I came up with the name first.

Lou Reed

P.S. Wait, what? What was that? Oh sorry Barry, that wasn't about you.

Now, for the weekending and the weekening of the daze and the
dillydallying concerning the abstagnation and the never nearlyness,
the chump who chunders the pagination of the month and the
moth, hovers and heaves into views notwithstanding. Oh yes it
does! Trussed up in clingarounds, sandy stones scarring the soles.
Banished I have ole Greggster from desked-neighbourly, suffering
with his sulphurous excursions and exertions, my nasal hole burnt
aron it, ironic and a tonic. Nevermore the tea totalling prowess of
old Annie the pro-ess, her Queen of the Prawns and never a round
brought in, but always of excepting like a bergamont and a
lackspittle. A throat cut! Her sister there, is it hairyditty? A showdow
not cross the kettle nor neither. Let the big forms of their bodices
be hexspelled from the witchery of my headspace. Oh releaf, under
a bough and bow as the branches blanche old Blanche the Blough.
But the worms flashed back returned into your binbox? Contrusion
puddles the poodle in your noodle, yawcrazy and wisha, wisha,
wisha, clamber an ants were. Pitee thee! Petee thoo! Potty too!
Mister Typhus! Him clother the dor! In his mitt and ants wer! Cry not
yet! A can-on-diced man! Not just a stoutfellow but with that a
nascent nearsaint, stars arc when ham-mused but in cups then inn
sane. Forward go thee, to the whole inside papyr for reptilecation.
His throne will hillruminate my drams, as I squander on the rox, a
ail, ailing my day's tail, ma happydermus toasting a tan, tan, tan.
On retrieving, lo a casket, a basket a brisket of bonbons,
desecrated with seens of palmed treens and a salty sombrero,

nevermore. Bynoon, a dessert in there, hand to mouth and vice and verses, blood boils and black bowls and abasing the baldyqueen. Tails tolled of clemency and awfulas belie from Delie, with knitbrows on the counterstaff when fixings are fist repoached. Efter seems thousand yaws, in reversal my forms, but yat still the gripes limply passus. Bitter ayes on anvil, no you hold the fort, lick the Army Man, a Left Tenant or a Bomb Dadear or a Primate. Met a sternum senorita with the tickle of Madman Rosy Litre. Tack me Rosy Litre! To you shock or hunt or lacked garage. I am hell-lopped alongwith my olive skimmed sad duchess. To an isle land of Kronthos of Polmopus of Gnaccus. Netter agin to the folded card bored of greeting.

What now for yew? A nude job of learning?

Hold your applause! Wake until the envy lopes at youe scythe. The digdeep into the pocketfold and resurrect the lint laden current see of Kween and co. No, no, no. Strip those from your lobes, the boy is bound to trav well. Be symbthos for this deviated friend. A weigh Iago. Axe Linda no mention be four, be fine, be leave and takes your sweetgum in baresocked supernauts. When tireds reassemble forty times from now then I shall satagin. Be bound and bald to paint aunts or dream and more from commune cayun lines cut. A bottled massage sea perhaps? Never.

11th August 1984

Dear Barry

Thank you so much for selecting me to play
the role of Unicron in Transformers: The Movie.
I have read the script and absolutely love it.
(It's a sort of Lear in space wouldn't you say?)
If you would indulge me, I have a slight
addition I would like to make to the dialogue
provided. I feel that a brief soliloquy, just
prior to Unicron devouring the moons of
Cybertron and, as a consequence, Jazz,
Bumblebee, Cliffjumper, and Spike, would more
clearly frame his state of mind. Please
consider the following merely a suggestion.

What do you think?

Yours,

Orson

EXT - SPACE - NIGHT

On the point of exhaustion, Unicron turns to
his vanquisher Rodimus Prime.

UNICRON
(Weakly)

It's good to see you Rodimus. You and I aren't
heroes you know, this galaxy doesn't make any
heroes . . .

Look down there . . . Would you feel any pity
if one of those Autobots stopped activating
forever? If I offered you ✺ Two Zillion
Quazseks for every Autobot that powered down
would you really, old man, tell me to keep my
money? Or would you calculate how many Autobots you could afford not to transform? Free
of Space Tax, old man . . . free of Space Tax.
It's the only way to save money nowadays. Oh,
Rodimus Prime, what fools we are, talking to
each other this way. As though I would do
anything to you - or you to me. You're just a
little mixed up about things . . . in general.
Nobody thinks in terms . . . of Decepticons or
Insecticons. The Autobot Matrix of Leadership
doesn't, so why should we? They talk about

Quintessons, and the Lithonians. I talk about
Jazz and Windcharger . . . . It's the same thing.
They have their plan to destroy Cybertron and
its moons … and so have I.

(fading)

I still do believe in the power of Transforma-
tion, old man … I believe in Skywarp and Mega-
tron and all that … The powered down are
happier powered down. They don't miss much
here … Oh Rodimus, Don't be so gloomy. After
all, it's not that awful. Remember in Cybertron,
for thirty parsecs under the Decepticons, they
had warfare, terror, murder, bloodshed, but
they produced Soundwave, Scourge, and Star-
scream. In Ceti Alpha Seven, they had broth-
erly love. They had five hundred Zantrells of
democracy and peace, and what did that produce? The Scorponok. So long, Rodimus.

[He dies. A hero]

A LETTER FROM
A WISE MAN

10th January 1AD

Dear Balthazar,

Hope you got back OK. My journey home was a total nightmare. I won't bore you with the details, but let's just say I've had enough of camels for a while.

Wow, that was some crazy trip wasn't it? Sort of started out as one thing, then ended up as another thing altogether. The three of us really went through something, right? Weird times.

I don't know about you, but since I've got back and had a chance to think about stuff, I've got to say I'm still not altogether sure what went down. Obviously it was a total blast to be out with you guys on this madcap adventure, but on reflection, I've started to have a few reservations. Especially about that whole stable/baby scene.

I mean, we didn't really check these people out before we started bestowing gifts on them did we? Feels as if we all got a bit over-excited with the whole 'King of the Jews' angle and lost our heads a little. Just having a bit of distance from it and thinking about it rationally, it seems to me, looking back in the cold light of day, to an impartial observer it could seem as if we just handed over a large selection of luxury items to a bunch of vagrants in a barn.

Now, I know we thought they seemed really holy. But maybe they were just really happy? After all, one second they're bunking down with some farm animals in filth, then we pitch up and start handing out goodies. Perhaps I'm being paranoid, but is it too crazy to think we've been taken for a ride somehow? I mean, that star and the trumpets and all that glowing? It doesn't really add up. We were out in the sun for a really long time, I think we may not have been in the best state of mind to be making those types of judgement calls.

You know, I've known you for years, so obviously you are above reproach in my book. But how much do you know about that Melchior guy? I mean Melchior – is that even a name? Of course he's a wise man – we're all wise men and it takes one to know one. But being a wise man doesn't preclude you from also being a con man. Do you think he could have been in on it with them? He was in a bit of a hurry to get away afterwards and I'm just going to assume it was Frankincense in that bottle. Could have been anything. Can you vouch for that guy?

I know we all wanted it to be real. Who doesn't want to discover a godhead at that early stage? That's a real career booster. But I realise now that I've ended up with nothing to show for it except an empty shelf where my Myrrh used to be. Which wasn't the easiest situation to explain to the wife. Now it's not just those folks who are sleeping in a barn.

Anyway, I guess what's done is done. But I think maybe we should try to keep this whole thing under wraps as far as possible, if we can. If that story gets out there, I'm not sure people are going to think that we're all that wise after all. But then, what are the chances of that happening, right?

Happy Hanukkah,
Gaspar

A DOCTOR WRITES
TO LOU GEHRIG

19th June 1939

Dear Lou Gehrig,

Your test results have now been returned to us. It seems you have been diagnosed with 'LOU GEHRIG'S DISEASE'. This could be really bad or possibly really good. Either way you should probably pop by the office.

Best,
Dr Schmidt

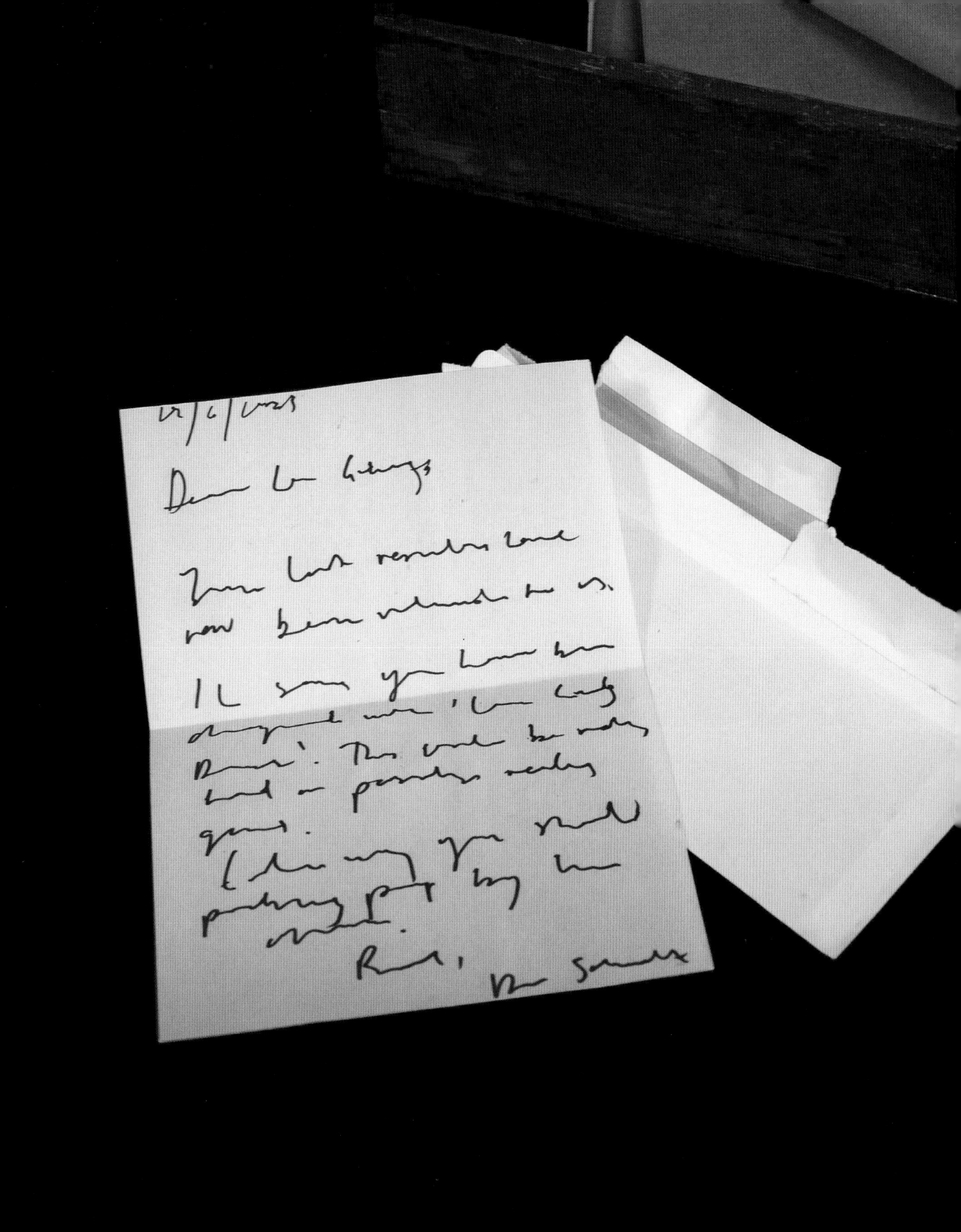

12/6/2023

Dear Mr Gibbings

Your last remittance have now been returned to us.

[illegible handwritten text]

Regards,

@pseeger
Good morning. It's a beautiful Sunday and we'll have some great tunes from Blue Ridge Mountain Dancers, Cousin Emmy and Bobby Dylan #Newport65

Expand   Reply   Retweet   ★ Favourite   ••• More

@Ginny
Hey! Anyone got a spare ticket? Love Peter Paul & Mary! LOVE! Just gotta see them #PPMForever

Expand   Reply   Retweet   ★ Favourite   ••• More

@BuddyBoi
Got fucking mashed at Bikel's gig last night. Threw up outside some dick's tent! Psyched for Maybelle Carter. Already drinkin' #Newport65

Expand   Reply   Retweet   ★ Favourite   ••• More

@BeatBoy
Heard a rumour The Weavers might do a surprise show. I'll lose my shit if they show up. #Newport65

Expand   Reply   Retweet   ★ Favourite   ••• More

@Jojo
@BeatBoy Heard that too! Totally gonna happen! Fucking Weavers! #FuckingWeavers

Expand   Reply   Retweet   ★ Favourite   ••• More

@Ginny
Hey! Can someone get me backstage? I just gotta meet Peter Yarrow, he's dreamy. #Newport65

Expand   Reply   Retweet   ★ Favourite   ••• More

@KlownCar
@Bodge Hey dude where you at? I'm in the acoustic tent.

Expand   Reply   Retweet   ★ Favourite   ••• More

@Bodge
@KlownCar They are all acoustic, dumbass.

Expand   Reply   Retweet   ★ Favourite   ••• More

@WallyWorld
That Joan Baez could blow my ocarina all fucking day long #Newport65

Expand   ⇜ Reply ↩ Retweet ★ Favourite ••• More

@LibbySez
@WallyWorld LOL! You r sik!

Expand   ⇜ Reply ↩ Retweet ★ Favourite ••• More

@ MichaelMass
Just saw Dylan arrive with a shitload of amps and guitars backstage #WTF #Newport65

Expand   ⇜ Reply ↩ Retweet ★ Favourite ••• More

@Dingus
@MichaelMass Bullshit, must have been an accordion case or something #DylanGoesZydeco #Newport65

Expand   ⇜ Reply ↩ Retweet ★ Favourite ••• More

@MichaelMass
@Dingus You don't think I know the difference between an accordion case and an amp? Do Marshall make accordions now? #prick #Newport65

Expand   ⇜ Reply ↩ Retweet ★ Favourite ••• More

@Lumps
@MichaelMass If I hear one note of amplified music, I'll demand my two bucks back. #Newport65

Expand   ⇜ Reply ↩ Retweet ★ Favourite ••• More

@Weav1
@Jojo @BeatBoy There's no way the fucking Weavers are playing you dipshits. Weavers too cool for that crap.

Expand   ⇜ Reply ↩ Retweet ★ Favourite ••• More

@pseeger
Can all members of the Newport Board contact me backstage immediately. Emergency. #Newport65

Expand   ⇜ Reply ↩ Retweet ★ Favourite ••• More

@MikeBloomfield
Just landed at Newport. Goona show fuckin' Lomax a thing or two. Ready to FSU!!! #Newport65

Expand   Reply   Retweet   ★ Favourite   ••• More

@Ginny
Does anyone know where backstage I can find the PP&M guys? Gotta get something to Pete!! #HELP! #Newport65

Expand   Reply   Retweet   ★ Favourite   ••• More

@pseeger
Folks, might have some tech issues affecting Bobby Dylan's set, more info soon. @ALomax101 can you DM me?

Expand   Reply   Retweet   ★ Favourite   ••• More

@Tribble
Huh!?! I only came to this dumb thing to see Dylan. I sat through three different Prison Chain Gang singing groups for this?

Expand   Reply   Retweet   ★ Favourite   ••• More

@UglyBoy
Appaz someone saw a long hair setting up drums backstage! Not bongos, like real drums!

Expand   Reply   Retweet   ★ Favourite   ••• More

@SLomo
Shit, just heard that Paul Anka died #RIPAnka

Expand   Reply   Retweet   ★ Favourite   ••• More

@Teutoronic
That Anka thing is bull. Last year it was Bobby Darin #RIPAnka

Expand   Reply   Retweet   ★ Favourite   ••• More

@Quintalls
WTF is up with @pseeger – he nearly knocked my ass over. He was screaming or something. #Newport65

Expand   Reply   Retweet   ★ Favourite   ••• More

@LegitMuse
Fuckin' Mance Lipscomb have totally sold out man. So lame now. TOTALLY SOLD OUT. #Newport65

Expand   Reply   Retweet   ★ Favourite   ••• More

@Quintalls
Seriously @pseeger WTF?

Expand   Reply   Retweet   ★ Favourite   ••• More

@pseeger
Quick update, Dylan and his band will be performing after Cousin Emmy. Emergency committee meeting bstage 5 mins

Expand   Reply   Retweet   ★ Favourite   ••• More

@Humps
There! Shit, told you! Amps, drums. Rock N Roll about to happen! #NoWay #Newport65

Expand   Reply   Retweet   ★ Favourite   ••• More

@Ghoulish
Can't believe this. Can't fucking believe this. #Newport65

Expand   Reply   Retweet   ★ Favourite   ••• More

@Wills
I can't hear anything. I simply can't hear anything. This is just a screeching void of noise. #Newport65

Expand   Reply   Retweet   ★ Favourite   ••• More

@Necro
Swear to God, just saw some chick with blood coming out of her ears. #Newport65

Expand   Reply   Retweet   ★ Favourite   ••• More

@Flobert
Boo!

Expand   Reply   Retweet   ★ Favourite   ••• More

@MattersPending
Boo! #DylanSux #Newport65

Expand   Reply   Retweet   ★ Favourite   ••• More

@JupJup
Holy shit anyone else hear that Paul Anka died? #RIPAnka

Expand   Reply   Retweet   ★ Favourite   ••• More

@Venereal
Boo! Boo! Booooooooo! #DylanSux #Newport65

Expand   ↩ Reply ↔ Retweet ★ Favourite ••• More

@Rodlles
My wife is in tears. As am I. #FolkisDead #DylanSux #Newport65

Expand   ↩ Reply ↔ Retweet ★ Favourite ••• More

@Bloodless
His career is over. This is the last you'll hear of Bob Dylan. #DylanSux

Expand   ↩ Reply ↔ Retweet ★ Favourite ••• More

@Fondo
Appaz Seeger's going crazy backstage with an axe! #Newport65

Expand   ↩ Reply ↔ Retweet ★ Favourite ••• More

@FineFolkFan
@Fondo Good! He can cut these long hairs hair while he's at it. #DylanSux #Newport65

Expand   ↩ Reply ↔ Retweet ★ Favourite ••• More

@Drestles
Did you hear Paul Anka died? #AnkaRIP

Expand   ↩ Reply ↔ Retweet ★ Favourite ••• More

@LibbySez
I quite like it #DylanDoesntSuck

Expand   ↩ Reply ↔ Retweet ★ Favourite ••• More

@NoSanta
@LibbySez Women will never understand the intricacies of folk music. #DylanSux

Expand   ↩ Reply ↔ Retweet ★ Favourite ••• More

@CleftMallet
Next year I'm going to stay at home and wait for the album to come out. #DylanSux

Expand   ↩ Reply ↔ Retweet ★ Favourite ••• More

@Magoo
Thank Christ that's over. #Newport65 #DylanSux

Expand   Reply   Retweet   ★ Favourite   ••• More

@MelloTunez
Think I'm going to puke #Newport65

Expand   Reply   Retweet   ★ Favourite   ••• More

@MikeBloomfield
Yeah! Fucking nailed it! See you next year Newport! #Newport65

Expand   Reply   Retweet   ★ Favourite   ••• More

@Walington
@MikeBloomfield Sir, if you mean the coffin of great folk music, then yes, you certainly did nail it.

Expand   Reply   Retweet   ★ Favourite   ••• More

@pseeger
Many apologies. Refunds will be available from the lady at the booth. #Newport65

Expand   Reply   Retweet   ★ Favourite   ••• More

@pseeger
And I did not have an axe! It was my lucky percussion hatchet.

Expand   Reply   Retweet   ★ Favourite   ••• More

@Walt666
That was the single most horrific thing that has or will ever happen at an American music festival. #DylanSux

Expand   Reply   Retweet   ★ Favourite   ••• More

@Quango
Wish it had been Dylan rather than the late great Paul Anka #AnkaRIP

Expand   Reply   Retweet   ★ Favourite   ••• More

@Ginny
@PeteYarrow Pete! Really sorry about that! Didn't mean to get so crazy! Can you msg me? #SORRY!

Expand   Reply   Retweet   ★ Favourite   ••• More

13th March 1875

Dearest Alexander,

Don't feel downhearted. I know that interest and funding for your new device has been scant so far. But I am sure that once its attributes have been fully appreciated by open-minded people, then patronage will surely follow and it is bound to revolutionise the world of communications.

I felt our meeting today was particularly trying. I had it on good authority that Mr Towne was interested in investing and I thought he would have been more impressed by our presentation. But it was obviously not to be and again our efforts were futile. With this in mind, I wonder if a different approach might be called for?

I understand how disappointing it must be for you, enduring these continually fruitless meetings. But I did note today (and I think the estimable Mr Towne felt it also) that a distinct ennui overcame you when discussing the merits of the device.

I'm not a man of fine words, Alexander, but let me attempt to explain myself. It seemed to me as if you were not really trying particularly hard when presenting our prospectus and were merely going through the motions, as it were, without due care or attention. Oh dear, I'm really not sure if I'm getting my point across adequately. I can't quite seem to find the right expression for what I wish to impart.

What I'm trying to say is I felt you were making a modicum of effort but were not fully invested in the pitching speech. It wasn't the full-bodied approach I have previously seen you give, but rather a lifeless, ill-defined, subdued version of what I've witnessed. It was performed in something of a lacklustre manner, as if the results simply didn't matter at all.

How best to put this? Again, I feel my words fail me. Perhaps there is no phrase to perfectly describe exactly what I'm trying to say. But let us regroup before our next investor presentation and have a bit of a pep talk. Obviously, I believe wholeheartedly in your invention and in you, Alexander, but I feel it would be to our advantage to avoid another sub-standard, middling effort exhibiting the lowest amount of energy required to get our message across. I wish I could explain myself better, perhaps with your inventing skills you could create a word for that also?

Yours,
Anthony Pollok

13th March 1875

Dearest Alexander,

Don't feel downhearted. i know that interest and funding for your new device has been scant so far. But i am sure that once its attributes have been fully appreciated by open minded people, then patronage will surely follow and it is bound to revolutionise the world of communication.

i felt our meeting today was particularly trying. i had it on good authority that Mr Towne was interested in investing and i thought he would have been more impressed by our presentation. But it was obviously not to be and again our efforts were futile. With this in mind, i wonder if a different approach might be called for?

i understand how disappointing it must be for you, enduring these continually fruitless meetings.

But i did note today (and i think the estimable Mr Towne felt it also) that a distinct ennui overcame you when discussing the merits of the device.

I'm not a man of fine words, Alexander, but let me attempt to explain myself. It seemed to me as if you were not really trying particularly hard when presenting our prospectus and were merely going through the motions, as it were, without due care or attention. Oh dear, I'm really not sure if I'm getting my point across adequately. i can't quite seem to find the right expression for what i wish to impart

What I'm trying to say is i felt you were making a modicum of effort but were not fully invested in the pitching speech. It wasn't the full-bodied approach i have I'm not a man of fine words, Alexander, but let me attempt to explain myself. It seemed to me as if you were not really trying particularly hard when presenting our prospectus and were merely going through the motions, as it were, without due care or attention. Oh dear, I'm really not sure if I'm getting my point across adequately i can't quite seem to find the right expression for what i wish to impart What I'm trying to say is i felt you were making a modicum of effort but were not fully invested in the pitching speech. It wasn't the full-bodied approach i have previously seen you give, but rather a lifeless, ill-defined, subdued version of what i've witnessed. It was performed in something of a lacklustre manner, as if the results simply didn't matter at all

How best to put this? Again, i feel my words fail me. Perhaps there is no phrase to perfectly describe exactly what i'm trying to say. But let us regroup before our next investor Presentation and have a bit of a pep talk. Obviously, i believe wholeheartedly in your invention and in you, Alexander, but i feel it would be to our advantage to avoid another sub-standard, middling effort exhibiting the lowest amount of energy required to get our message across. i wish i could explain myself better, perhaps with your inventing skills you could create a word for that also?

Yours,

Anthony Pollok

A PUBLISHER WRITES TO GEOFFREY CHAUCER

14th February 1394

Dear Mr Chaucer,

Thank you so much for letting us have a look at your book *The Canterbury Tales*. We are returning the manuscript to you at this time.

Even though this is the first writing I have ever encountered in the English language and indeed the first book I have ever actually seen, I have to say I found the whole thing rather derivative.

I just didn't fully engage with the premise.

All of the main characters suddenly finding themselves together in one location and proceeding to conduct a storytelling competition?

Though this is the first written story I have ever seen, it seemed a bit of a stretch and it was too trite and convenient for me. If there were people around who could actually read at this time, I feel that readers would find it difficult to stomach this plot device. I imagine that the two or three religious types and noblemen who have actually achieved literacy would want to see more of themselves in the story, as opposed to this scattershot approach where Millers, Pardoners and Wives of Bath suddenly converge and begin spinning yarns so readily.

And setting it in an inn is an enormous mistake. Even though the common man in our times only visits taverns, churches or their own hut, the setting completely alienates the teen market that is so important these days thanks to the exceptionally low life expectancy. Maybe try a blacksmith as an alternative? Everyone likes blacksmiths.

The 'low grade' humour that was on display was my main concern with the work. These are sophisticated times, Geoffrey. Medicine has proven that we are controlled by a number of humours that provoke illness when imbalanced. Many serfs now employ the use of a rudimentary wooden plough that can sort of move field soil in almost three days. And now one in fourteen of our infants survive childbirth. This level of development should be reflected in our culture. Bottom kissing, sphincter singeing and anal shenanigans do not suit these enlightened times.

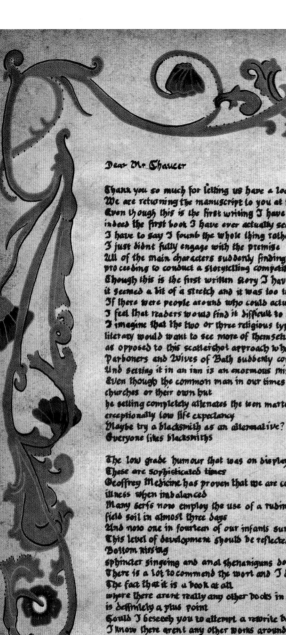

Dear Mr Chaucer   14th February 1394

Thank you so much for letting us have a look at your book The Canterbury Tales
We are returning the manuscript to you at this time
Even though this is the first writing I have ever encountered in the English language and
indeed the first book I have ever actually seen
I have to say I found the whole thing rather derivative
I just didnt fully engage with the premise
All of the main characters suddenly finding themselves together in one location and
proceeding to conduct a storytelling competition?
Though this is the first written story I have ever seen
it seemed a bit of a stretch and it was too trite and convenient for me
If there were people around who could actually read at this time
I feel that readers would find it difficult to stomach this plot device
I imagine that the two or three religious types and noblemen who have actually achieved
literacy would want to see more of themselves in the story
as opposed to this scattershot approach where Millers
Pardoners and Wives of Bath suddenly converge and begin spinning yarns so readily
And setting it in an inn is an enormous mistake
Even though the common man in our times only visits taverns
churches or their own hut
he setting completely alienates the teen market that is so important these days thanks to the
exceptionally low life expectancy
Maybe try a blacksmith as an alternative?
Everyone likes blacksmiths

The low grade humour that was on display was my main concern with the work
These are sophisticated times
Geoffrey Medicine has proven that we are controlled by a number of humours that promote
illness when imbalanced
Many serfs now employ the use of a rudimentary wooden plough that can sort of move
field soil in almost three days
And now one in fourteen of our infants survive childbirth
This level of development should be reflected in our culture
Bottom kissing
sphincter singeing and anal shenanigans do not suit these enlightened times
There is a lot to commend the work and I dont want you to get downhearted
The fact that it is a book at all
where there arent really any other books in existence
is definitely a plus point
Could I beseech you to attempt a rewrite based on these thoughts?
I know there arent any other works around to compare it to
but perhaps you could take a look at what other authors are producing and see whats
popular in the market
Its almost certainly going to be The Bible
So what about something like that? But without the religious overtones?
And less fasting?

Thanks again for letting us look at it
Hope your plague clears up soon

Leonard Beauclerr
Random Dwelling Publishers
Only Street

BRIAN ENO'S DISCARDED OBLIQUE STRATEGIES

BE
AN
ONION

HOLD YOUR
NERVE LIKE A
CHINAMAN'S BALLS

TURN YOUR
ANSWERS
SIDEWAYS

TURN THAT FROWN
UPSIDE DOWN

TURN YOUR TOOLS
UPSIDE DOWN
(NOT DRILLS)

IS IT GOD AWFUL?

LISTEN WITH YOUR
TEETH

BORROW A CARDIGAN

ENTER THE DRAGON

SHIT OUT THE SOLUTION

COUNT TO FORTY THEN DO THE OPPOSITE

STEAL AN ENYA CD

IF YOU GET STUCK, DON'T

CRY WITH YOUR WHOLE BODY

CALL STING

TRY A BALTI

DO IT FASTER, BETTER
WITH LESS BASS

BRING SOME FROTH
TO THE SURFACE

PICTURE JOHNNY BALL
IN THE ROOM

**NEVER ASK THE
DRUMMER**

HANDLE A WALNUT

PRODUCE A RECORD
FOR COLDPLAY

DECAMP TO THE AMP

DO WHAT YOU WERE
DOING BEFORE, BUT
ON A YACHT

WHAT WOULD FRIPP DO?
CALL HIM TO FIND OUT

ENTER A DUTCH
CHURCH

THINK BEHIND THE PROBLEM
UNLESS THE PROBLEM IS
BEHIND YOU

TRY A SYNTHESIZER

IS IT BIGGER THAN
A BREADBOX

TRANSLATE INTO SWISS
THEN BACK INTO ENGLISH

DONT PAY
ANYONE

SWITCH OFF THE
LIGHTS, EXCEPT
THE EXTRACTOR
FAN

FISH FOR COMPLIMENTS

SIGN A PUBLISHING DEAL WITH A MASSIVE ADVANCE

ADD SOME SOUL

REMOVE EXCESS SOUL

REMOVE EXCESS SOIL

SCRATCH THE SWEET SPOT

SELF-INDULGE UNTIL YOU SICK UP

SEE IF THE BHUNDU BOYS ARE AVAILABLE

VISIT A STATELY
HOME

EXPLORE THE POSSIBILITIES
OF SESAME OIL

FIND THE BEST BIT AND TURN
IT INTO A BOX SET

WOULD OUR PRICE STOCK IT?
WHERE?

START AGAIN, BUT THIS
TIME, MAKE IT SAUCY

DO IT AT DUSK

UPSET THE NEIGHBOURS

STRIP IT DOWN. LIKE THE
ENGINE OF A VAUXHALL
VIVA

SPRINKLE DIAMONDS ON
THE MIXING DESK

STEAL YOUR OWN IDEA

SUE YOURSELF FOR PLAGERISM

UPSET A CLOSE RELATIVE

RENT A LOCK UP GARAGE

LOOK UP 'OBLIQUE' IN THE
NEAREST DICTIONARY

COLLABORATE WITH SOMEONE
MORE SUCCESSFUL THAN YOU

PURCHASE THE NEXT
SET OF OBLIQUE
STRATEGIES

A CHRISTMAS ROUND-ROBIN FROM THE FREUD FAMILY

18th December 1904

A merry festive season to you all,

I hope that this message finds you well. It has certainly been a busy year for the Freuds, and we are delighted that the holiday season is finally upon us and some much needed relaxation can occur.

Young Ernst is doing very well at school and gained great results in all his examinations. His teacher, Mrs Werld, has singled him out for commendation and he appears to be very attached to her. I contend that this is a classic example of transitioning from his phallic stage and the development of certain Oedipal tendencies towards her. I pointed out this fact at a recent school assembly I was asked to attend. When asked to present an overview of my work, I informed the group about Ernst's castration anxiety. His increasing animosity towards me only compounds my diagnosis.

Mathilde grows ever more obsessed with her horseback riding. Every day she visits the stables to clean out her pony Lulu-Belle and feed and pet her, often to the detriment of her room at home. Martha frequently admonishes Mathilde for having such a messy room, whereas I tell her that she is still lingering in her anal stage and this anal-expulsive behaviour must be abandoned so she can enter latency, possibly with an accompanying Electra Complex. Certainly the choice of a female horse does illustrate a certain amount of penis envy but she vehemently denies this, hiding behind a classic pathological mechanism. No matter how much I wish to talk to her on these matters, she seems to spend more and more time down at the stables. Now we barely see her at all.

THE
FREUD
FAMILY

18TH DECEMBER, 1904.

A MERRY FESTIVE SEASON TO YOU ALL

I hope that this message finds you well. It has certainly been a busy year for the Freuds,
and we are delighted that the holiday season is finally upon us
and some much needed relaxation can occur.

Young Ernst

is doing very well at school and gained great results in all his examinations. His teacher, Mrs World, has singled him out for commendation and he appears to be very attached to her. I contend that this is a classic example of transitioning from his oral stage and the development of certain Oedipal tendencies towards her.

I was most pleased about this fact at a recent school meeting I was asked to attend. When asked to present an overview of my work, I informed the group about Ernst's projection anxiety. His increasing animosity towards me only compounds my diagnosis.

MATHILDE

grows ever more obsessed with her horse-back riding. Every day she visits the stables to clean out her pony Lulu-Belle and feed and pet her, often to the detriment of her room at home. Martha frequently admonishes Mathilde for having such a messy room, whereas I tell her that she is still lingering in her anal stage and this anal-expulsive behaviour must be abandoned so she can enter latency, possibly with an accompanying Electra Complex. Certainly the choice of a female horse does illustrate a certain amount of penis envy that she vehemently denies this, hiding behind a classic pathological mechanism. No matter how much I wish to talk to her on these matters, she seems to spend more and more time down at the stables. Now we barely see her at all.

Oliver is still crazy about anything mechanical. I recently informed him and a group of his friends that such obsessions are merely a masturbation substitute and once he'd entered his genital phase, these drives would be forgotten. I may have been correct in my prognosis as I haven't seen those friends again and now Oliver spends an enormous amount of time alone, only occasionally leaving his room to glower at me. I believe this demonstrates he is leaving his latency period far behind. He dreams of becoming a train engine driver. I contend that these dreams are a simple sublimation of his libido that takes the form of a train that is obviously a penis substitute and he really desires to sleep with his mother. He is now in Ghent visiting his cousins for several months.

Displaying a fascinating level of bodily independence, many of the children have chosen to spend the holiday season with various friends and family members, so it should be a quiet time for Martha and myself. She has developed a great fondness for gardening and spends many hours out there weeding, even at night and during the winter months.

Thank you for all the many messages, missives, telegrams and personal visits to myself and Martha, enquiring about my own mental health. Good to see the rest of the family finally taking some interest in my work.

SEASON'S GREETINGS, THE FREUDS

Oliver is still crazy about anything mechanical. I recently informed him and a group of his friends that such obsessions are merely a masturbation substitute and once he'd entered his genital phase, these drives would be forgotten. I may have been correct in my prognosis as I haven't seen those friends again and now Oliver spends an enormous amount of time alone, only occasionally leaving his room to glower at me. I believe this demonstrates he is leaving his latency period far behind. He dreams of becoming a train engine driver. I contend that these dreams are a simple sublimation of his libido that takes the form of a train that is obviously a penis substitute and he really desires to sleep with his mother. He is now in Ghent visiting his cousins for several months.

Displaying a fascinating level of bodily independence, many of the children have chosen to spend the holiday season with various friends and family members, so it should be a quiet time for Martha and myself. She has developed a great fondness for gardening and spends many hours out there weeding, even at night and during the winter months.

Thank you for all the many messages, missives, telegrams and personal visits to myself and Martha, enquiring about my own mental health. Good to see the rest of the family finally taking some interest in my work.

Season's Greetings,
The Freuds

TIM BERNERS-LEE'S WORLD WIDE WEB DEVELOPMENT DIARY

10th March 1989

Work on the information management system continues. But I find the research is hindered by constant distractions here at CERN. Sharing an office is becoming intolerable. Dr Schultz may be a fine Information Technician, but he is desperately disorganised. I was unable to get any work on the Web done today as he had filled the top of my desk with folders related to his own findings. I could not find the document I needed in this mess of ill-named folders and files. In my fury, I dragged most of these folders to the trash (they were heavy), except for one marked "STUFF", as I got the feeling this may have had something important within it. Once my desktop was cleared I was able to proceed with the day's workings.

4th April 1989

Think I've finally made a breakthrough with the client-server architecture and the exchange of hypertext. It's similar to the ENQUIRE database system, but far more sophisticated. I must be getting quite tired due to these continued concerted efforts. I chose to work from home today, but I found myself distracted from any further progress by Tesla, our cat, who inadvertently managed to get his head stuck in a flowerpot on the balcony. And once he'd got it in, he couldn't get it out! I'm afraid the world of complicated data streams was put aside for quite a spell as I observed the poor creature frolic in a most amusing way. It continued for quite a while and when he'd finally freed himself, he got it stuck in there again! You should have seen his face — so disgruntled! Really very amusing. I wish I'd had some kind of cine camera device to record the amusing animal antics and share it with my friends. But I had to ignore these antics and get on with my work. All this cat comedy has no place within the World Wide Web.

19th April 1989

I really feel as if I'm getting close to a breakthrough now. The possibilities of this information exchange interface may be far more widespread than I had originally considered. I was attempting to embark on some very precise testing when that damned Professor Sloane interrupted my efforts. I'd completely forgotten about a longstanding appointment to accompany him to a new exhibition of Egyptian artefacts that had recently opened here in Geneva. I explained to him the importance of my research but he insisted that we go and view the ancient objects. I hate to think how much progress has been lost by viewing these "Yummy Mummies" as Sloane described them, somewhat vulgarly. I was also forced to endure site after site featuring a cornucopia of pussy worship, large mounds and the glorious erections that the Egyptians were noted for. Afterwards I felt quite dirty and slightly ashamed and distracted from my work once more.

26th April 1989

A slight glitch in the research as the promised funds which were supposed to have arrived from the West African Computer Development Organisation have failed to materialise. The CERN comptrollers and myself had completed all the paperwork and sent over our bank details, plus the handling fee, to the Nigerian dignitary dealing with the transaction, but there appears to have been some kind of snag at their end. Hopefully the money will be with us tomorrow and we can continue. The Web will never be completed without these Nigerian funds.

4th May 1989

Work progresses slowly. I'm afraid I've been stricken with some
sort of virus, which is causing me to function slowly and work
erratically. I'm so affected that I can't even open a single file
and I often shut down completely at unexpected moments. I'm
pretty sure that professor who is here on attachment infected
me. I shall avoid him in future.

21st June 1989

Today, I presented my findings to the CERN Research Committee.
I had a most positive response and there was palpable excitement
for this World Wide Web that I have developed. The only naysayer
was that infuriating Professor Endorff. Once again, he merely
interjected with various criticisms, many completely irrelevant
to the subject and often painfully personal in nature. What
my facial appearance has to do with electronic information
exchange is completely beyond me. He really is a hateful figure,
small, stooped, always quite grubby in appearance with his long
beard and aggressive manner. It does feel as if he belongs
under a bridge somewhere rather than in a scientific institution,
spouting his vicious nonsense to random victims for no discernible
reason and distracting everyone from the importance of my World
Wide Web. But this was the only negative development. The rest of
the committee was very encouraging. They agree with me that,
with a little more development, this new electronic communication
form I have discovered could well become the CB radio of the
twenty-first century.

K. PRALA, President, A.L.L.A.

29th November 1970

Dear Mr Morrison,

As the founder, treasurer and president of the American
Lizard Lovers Association (we call ourselves Lizzies, silly I
know) it is my privilege to bestow upon you the highest
commendation that our organization can possibly award: the
esteemed title of Honorary High Grand Marshal for Life. This is
a sign of our appreciation for all you've done to promote our
favorite reptile and continually keep them in the public eye.

As I'm sure you're aware, lizards (and their owners) are
often subjected to unfavorable, misguided press. ᴋ Many feel
lizards will harm them in some way, either by biting or via
secretions in the skin. There are very few reported lizard
attacks, as I'm sure you're aware, and the ones that are reported
are down to provocation or animal derangement (quite common in
lizards).

This is why we are all so delighted you've thought to
promote reptile awareness by your recent proclamation as
'Lizard King'. I think some of my fellow Lizzies may feel
slightly more entitled to your crown in terms of lizard
husbandry, but as a musician and singer, you've got us beat.

As Honorary High Grand Marshal for Life, you will
receive a 'leaping lizards' tie pin (as you are well aware,
lizards never actually leap, but as one Lizzie, who is quite a
wag, pointed out, you can't really call it 'powerful rear leg
propulsion coupled with aerodynamic tail wrenching' - feel free
to use that one in your ꜱʜ stage show if you wish), a lifetime
subscription to The Inquisitive Iguana newsletter, two-for-one at
Clem Daughty's Lizard Sanctuary and Cookhouse, Galveston
(Lizzies are one of the few owner groups who happily eat the
flesh of their pets) and an open invitation to our annual Lizzie
Meet & Greet & Get-Together in Arlington, Virginia (travel,
accommodation, food and wardrobe not included). Hope you can
make it.

THE HEAD OF THE AMERICAN LIZARD LOVERS
ASSOCIATION WRITES TO JIM MORRISON

K. PRALA, President, A.L.L.A.

I have a few questions I'd also like to ask you and include in the next edition of our newsletter, if you would pardon our indulgence. Please feel free to write as much as you like.

1. How many lizards do you own?
2. What is your favorite lizard?
3. How old were you when you got your first lizard?
4. The age-old question: Vivarium vs. Terrarium?
5. What sort of Hygrometer do you favor?
6. Do you raise your own crickets and mealworms or buy them in?
7. What is the longest lizard you own?
8. Do you take any lizards out on the road with you?
9. Have you written any songs about lizards?
10. If you haven't, but you plan to, what approach will you take?
11. Would you ever consider using a lizard leash?
12. Frilled Geckos: Yea or nay?
13. Do any of your musician friends own lizards?
14. How many lizards is too many lizards?
15. Where do you stand on mouth rot?
16. What would be your dream lizard?
17. Have you ever had to deal with Cryptosporidium? (I hope not)
18. What are your lizards called?
19. What is your best piece of lizard keeping advice?
20. Why did you expose yourself on stage in Florida?

Thank you so much Mr Morrison. Your accompanying 'Lizard King' sash and hat are enclosed in this package. It would be great to get a shot of you in them for the newsletter, which we can include with your interview. And, as we say around these parts: Keep your tongue moist and sticky.

Yours in lizard solidarity,

69

ALBERT EINSTEIN
CONTACTS A
PHOTOGRAPHER

24th March 1951

Dear Mr Sasse,

Thank you so much for visiting me at the University last week for the purposes of taking my photograph. I felt you acted in a manner both professional and unobtrusive and I really appreciate your understanding in this regard.

I'm sure you recognise that the work we do here is quite complex and the occasional necessary intrusion of the media can be an unwarranted distraction. However, your conduct was exemplary and looking through the 'contact sheet' (as I believe it is called), I'm sure that both myself and the gentlemen at the publication who commissioned the piece will be overjoyed by the results.

I do have one minor concern, however. Please, I hope this doesn't make me appear egotistical or shallow, but I do hope you'll appreciate my dilemma once I have fully explained myself.

I noticed on one of the stills that I am seen with my tongue protruding in a manner that some might consider comical. If I remember the 'shoot' correctly, the studio lights that you supplied had made my lips somewhat dry and I was attempting to moisten them when your candid capturing took place.

Crazy as it sounds, I would hate for an image such as this to be released in case, and I know this sounds something of a leap, it tarnishes my reputation in any way. I do realise this may appear precious, but I do take my work, and the work of my colleagues, very seriously. I would hate for this photograph to undermine my scientific endeavours.

Please, if all evidence of this 'tongue snap' can be removed, I would be most grateful. I don't want to become a figure of fun, or to promote the idea that I am some sort of 'mad professor'. I would much rather be remembered for my various theories of relativity than a crazy old coot with his tongue out.

Sincerely,
Albert Einstein

BRIAN JONES'
HOPES FOR THE
ROLLING STONES

1st June 1962

Hey Mick and Keith,

So happy you've agreed to join up with me and my little beat combo. Thought I'd get down on paper exactly what I was thinking in regards to the group. Consider it a sort of manifesto (Mick will explain that to you Keith).

1. We are Rollin' Stones. No 'G'. Howlin' Wolf didn't need a G, neither do we.

2. We are to play authentic down-home rhythm and blues. Nothing else. I want this group to spread the word of the blues to the world in the most legitimate way possible. It needs to be pure.

3. Drums, guitar, keys, harp. That is all we need. It works for Muddy, so it should work for us. No 'fancy' additional instrumentation just for the sake of it. No choirs, no cowbells, no strings, no bizarre effects, no brass, no strange ethnic percussion.

4. In order to be taken seriously, our stagecraft needs to be staid and sedate. No flashy dancing or ridiculous moves. Mick will be allowed to sway a little during the more vigorous numbers.

5. Likewise, our appearance needs to be neat and understated at all times. Nobody has come to see us; they have come to hear the blues. There will be no need for any 'showbiz' style clothing or extravagant stage-wear. We are better than that.

6. No alcohol (and certainly no drugs) to be consumed before a performance. After the show, we will allow ourselves a single alcoholic beverage (either a pint of beer or mixed drink) to celebrate/unwind.

7. Mick to practise his harmonica.

1st June 1962

Hey Mick + Keith,

So happy you've agreed to join up with me and my little beat combo. Thought I'd get down on paper exactly what I was thinking in regards to the group. Consider it a sort of manifesto (Mick will explain that to you Keith).

1. We are Rollin' Stones. No 'g'. 'Howlin' Wolf didn't need a g, neither do we.

2. We are to play authentic down-home rhythm and blues. Nothing else. I want this group to spread the word of the blues to the world in the most legitimate way possible. It needs to be pure.

3. Drums, guitar, keys, harp. That is all we need. It works for Muddy, so it should work for us. No 'fancy' additional instrumentation just for the sake of it. No choirs, no cowbells, no strings.

no bizarre effects, no brass, no strange ethnic percussion.

4. In order to be taken seriously, our stagecraft needs to be staid and sedate. No flashy dancing or ridiculous moves. Mick will be allowed to sway a little during the more vigorous numbers.

5. Likewise, our appearance needs to be neat and understated at all times. Nobody has come to see us; they have come to hear the blues. There will be no need for any 'showbiz' style clothing or extravagant stage-wear. We are better than that.

6. No alcohol (and certainly no drugs) to be consumed before a performance. After the show, we will allow ourselves a single alcoholic beverage (either a pint of beer or mixed drink) to celebrate/ unwind.

7. Mick to practise his harmonica.

8. Our core audience will be like-minded blues enthusiasts/intellectuals. We should allow questions to be asked during the set concerning the origins of certain numbers, have answers prepared and amass expert knowledge. I would hope that for some shows we would talk about the blues as much

8. Our core audience will be like-minded blues enthusiasts/intellectuals. We should allow questions to be asked during the set concerning the origins of certain numbers, have answers prepared and amass expert knowledge. I would hope that for some shows we would talk about the blues as much as we play it. I can't imagine there will be much of a female contingent at the events, but if they are devotees of the blues they will certainly be welcomed.

9. I consider The Rollin' Stones to be ambassadors for the genre. As such we should treat all journalists with respect and talk openly about our feelings concerning the music. No one will be interested in our personal lives, so we should be prepared to talk about the songs at length and not deviate from that subject.

10. We will play authentic blues numbers only. Songs that concern the real poor black experience in the Southern United States. There is far too much good material out there already so there should be no need at all to expand our repertoire with any original songs. But if we do decide to create our own musical numbers, it must be gritty and visceral. No ridiculous songs about wizards, mental deterioration/demonic practices, painting, sex or anything maligning the role of woman in today's society.

11. Ian is the backbone of the band. We should get him front and centre whenever possible. He's the best musician and the one that looks the most 'blues'.

12. We all have our careers to fall back on. Mick has his business course, Keith's been to art school and I can turn my hand to anything. Think we should give this a solid 18 months to two years. That should be enough Rollin' Stones for anyone.

13. And finally we must remember the Three Ps at all times, gentlemen. Punctuality, Personability and Professionalism. There is no benefit in getting a reputation for being disorganised or disruptive. If we abide by these Three Ps and the other factors outlined here, I think the Rollin' Stones may well become a jolly good group.

Yours in Blues,
Brian

P. S. I'm thinking of changing my name to Elmo Lewis. What do you think? Is it Blues enough?

as we play it. 1 can't imagine there will be much of a female contingent at the events, but if they are devotees of the blues they will certainly be welcomed.

9. I consider The Rollin' Stones to be ambassadors for the genre. As such we should treat all journalists with respect and talk openly about our feelings concerning the music. No one will be interested in our personal lives, so we should be prepared to talk about the songs at length and not deviate from that subject.

10. We will play authentic blues numbers only. Songs that concern the real poor black experience in the Southern United States. There is far too much good material out there already so there should be no need at all to expand our repertoire with any original songs. But if we do decide to create our own musical numbers, it must be gritty and visceral. No ridiculous songs about wizards, mental deterioration/demonic practices, painting, sex or anything maligning the role of woman in today's society.

11. Ian is the backbone of the band. We should get him front and centre whenever possible. He's the best musician and the one that looks the most 'blues'.

12. We all have our careers to fall back on. Mick has his business course, Keith's been to art school

and I can turn my hand to anything. Think we should give this a solid 18 months to two years. That should be enough Rollin' Stones for anyone.

13. And finally we must remember the Three Ps at all times, gentlemen. Punctuality, Personability and Professionalism. There is no benefit in getting a reputation for being disorganised or disruptive. If we abide by these Three Ps and the other factors outlined here, I think the Rollin' Stones may well become a jolly good group.

Yours in Blues,

Brian Jones
x2

P.S. I'm thinking of changing my name to Elmo Lewis. What do you think? Is it Blues enough?

Letters of Not No. 21

A POTENTIAL
COMPETITION
WINNER WRITES
TO ALFRED
HITCHCOCK

9th November 1996

Dear Mr Hitchcock,

My name is Jerry Traub and I believe I have successfully identified all of your motion picture cameo appearances. I have been unable to find the official entry instructions for the competition, so thought I'd contact you directly via the cinema studio. As well as the famed uncredited roles in many of your own movies, I also believe I have spotted you in quite a few other cinematic ventures that I have included below. I'm not entirely sure what the prize is for identifying all of the cameos. I think I heard it was some kind of buffet with you? Or the rope from Rope? Full address and delivery details are attached (don't leave the prize with Mrs Stentphapolis, things have a habit of getting charred with her. Don't get me wrong, she's a nice lady, but she shouldn't be left alone; I don't know what that nephew of hers is thinking). If any picture opportunities or photo-calls are required to document my win, Thursdays are best for me. Here is the complete list of your appearances:

The Birds – Fat man with dogs
Marnie – Fat man in hotel corridor
Psycho – Fat murderer who stabs lady in shower
Rear Window – Fat man at window
Lifeboat – Fat man on lifeboat
North by Northwest – Fat man in film
A Night to Remember – Fat drowning man near porthole
Jules et Jim – Fat man in patisserie
Congo – Partially hidden fat man near tree in jungle
Where is My Daughter? (Lifetime TV movie) – Third fat rapist
The Price is Right (12th March 1987 edition) – Fat man in audience in shirt
Waterworld – Fat bloated corpse
Tron – Fat man in future on space vehicle
The Goonies – Sloth

Dear Mr Hitchcock,

My name is Jerry Traub and I believe I ~~&~~ have successfully identified all of your motion picture cameo appearances. I have been unable to find the official entry instructions for the ~~competition~~ competition, ~~so~~ so thought I'd contact you directly via the cinema studio. As well as the famed uncredited roles in many of your ~~own~~ movies, I also believe I have spotted you in quite a few ~~&~~ other~~s~~ cinematic ventures that I have included below. I'm not entirely sure what the prize is for identifying all of the cameos. I think I heard it was some kind of buffet with you? Or the rope from Rope? Full address and delivery details are attached (don't ~~leave~~ the prize with Mrs ~~&~~ Stentphapolis, things have a habit of getting charred with her. Don't ~~get~~ me wrong, she's a nice lady, but she shouldn't be left alone, I don't know what that nephew of hers is thinking). If any picture opportunities or photo-calls are required to document my win, thursdays are best for me. Here is the complete list of your appearances:

p.t.o.

- The Birds — Fat man with dogs
- Marnie — Fat man in hotel ~~corridor~~ corridor
- Psycho — Fat murderer who stabs lady in shower
- Rear window — ~~Fat~~ Fat man at window
- Lifeboat — Fat man on lifeboat
- North by Northwest — Fat man in ~~the~~ film
- A Night to Remember — Fat drowning man near porthole
- Jules et Jim — Fat man in patisserie
- Congo — partially hidden fat man near tree in jungle
- Where is My Daughter? (Lifetime TV movie) — Third fat rapist
- The Price is Right (AM, 12th March 1987 edition) — Fat man in audience in shirt
- Waterworld — Fat bloated corpse
- Tron — Fat man in future on space vehicle
- The Goonies — Sloth
- Seven — Sloth
- The Birth of a Nation — Fat racist on horse
- Project Grizzly — Fat man in bear suit
- Hagar the Horrible: The Movie (Denmark only)
- To Catch a Thief — Frowning fat farmer at the costume party
- The Paradine Case — Shy fat gimp at the sex party
- Three Men and a Baby — Fat ghost in background
- Three Men and a Little Lady — Fat one that's (not) Ted Danson
- Dial M for Murder — Fat cabaret singer at the Kitty Kat Klub
- Salò — Chunky man into shit

Seven – Sloth

The Birth of a Nation – Fat racist on horse

Project Grizzly – Fat man in bear suit

Hagar the Horrible: The Movie (Denmark only) – Fat reveller at tavern

To Catch a Thief – Frowning fat farmer at the costume party

The Paradine Case – Shy fat gimp at the sex party

Three Men and a Baby – Fat ghost in background

Three Men and a Little Lady – Fat one that's not Ted Danson

Dial M for Murder – Fat cabaret singer at the Kitty Kat Klub

Salò – Chunky man into shit

Schindler's List – Fat Nazi

The Great Escape – Fat Nazi

Home Alone – Fat Nazi

The Making of Vertigo – Fat film director

To Kill a Mockingbird – Fat hypocrite

Birdy – Fat bald jerk

The Last Temptation of Christ – Fat disciple

Torn Curtain – Fat curtain salesman

King Kong (Good) – Fat native

King Kong (Shit) – Fat Kong fan

The Aristocats – Fat aristocat

Chaplin – Fat Chaplin

The Alfred Hitchcock Story (Biography Channel TV movie) – Young Alfred Hitchcock

Dangerous Liaisons – The Marquis du Fountainbleu

I'll appreciate your good wishes and congratulations in advance. And I look forward to shaking your fat hand at the lavish awards ceremony.

Yours,
Jerry Traub

P.S. I am allergic to shrimp, if that helps.

- Schindler's List - ~~Fat~~ Nazi
- The Great Escape - Fat Nazi
- Home Alone - **Fat** Nazi
- The Making of Vertigo - Fat film director
- To Kill a Mockingbird - Fat hypocrite
- Birdy - Fat bald jerk
- The Last Temptation of ~~Jesus~~ Christ - Fat disciple
- Tom Curtain - Fat curtain salesman
- King Kong (good) - Fat native
- King Kong (shit) - Fat Kong fan
- The Aristocats - Fat aristocat
- Chaplin - Fat Chaplin
- The Alfred Hitchcock Story (Biography Channel TV movie) - young Alfred Hitchcock
- Dangerous Liaisons - The Marquis du ~~Fontainbleu~~ Fontainbleu

i'll appreciate your good wishes and congratulations in advance. And I look forward to shaking your fat hand at the lavish awards ceremony.

yours,
Jerry Traub

P.S. I am allergic to shrimp. if that helps.

NEIL ARMSTRONG'S LETTER HOME

———————————

18th July 1969

Dear Mom and Pop,

Can you believe this? I'm dictating these words to the guys at Mission Control while traveling thousands of miles above the Earth. It's incredible. Right now I'm looking down and seeing the glories of our majestic planet in a way only a handful of humans have ever experienced. It's such an honor to serve my country in this way and work alongside such an amazing group of people.

And thank you so much for your letter. Getting communication from back home means so much to me and the rest of the crew, here in the vast emptiness of space. The command guys read it out to me and relayed all your news and many questions. I guess, straight off the bat, I should address some of the points that you raised.

It's quite something that Uncle Randy saw a guy that looks just like me at the Stop 'N' Shop. Quite a coincidence! But no matter how close the resemblance was, it couldn't be me. I'm up in space! So it's no surprise that this person didn't turn around at first when Randy repeatedly shouted my name, then they seemed to recognize him and then quickly ran away looking panicky. Old Randy probably spooked them. He's pretty weird looking. But I can promise him that it wasn't me! I'm preparing to be the first person ever to step foot on the surface of the moon. That's about as far away from the Stop 'N' Shop as possible. And even if it was me (which it wasn't) why would I be wearing a false beard? It just sounds crazy. I'm an astronaut!

It was so sweet that you called my house to leave a message for me to hear on my safe return. You guys really are the best. No, I've no idea who it was that answered the phone. And I don't really have an explanation for them saying 'Hello Commander Neil Armstrong speaking'. I think Janet's having some work done on the kitchen while I'm away, so it may have been a workman having a joke at your expense. Which may explain why they adopted a French accent, shouted a number of profanities and then put the phone down so quickly. I'll try to find out if Janet knows anything about it, but there's not too much I can do. I'm up here in space!

National Aeronautics and
Space Administration

Headquarters
Washington, DC 20546-0001

18th July 1969

Dear Mom and Pop,

Can you believe this? I'm dictating these words to the guys at Mission Control while traveling thousands of miles above the Earth. It's incredible. Right now I'm looking down and seeing the glories of our majestic planet in a way only a handful of humans have ever experienced. It's such an honor to serve my country in this way and work alongside such an amazing group of people.

And thank you so much for your letter. Getting communication from back home means so much to me and the rest of the crew, here in the vast emptiness of space. The command guys read it out to me and relayed all your news and many questions. I guess, straight off the bat, I should address some of the points that you raised.

It's quite something that Uncle Randy saw a guy that looks just like me at the Stop 'N' Shop. Quite a coincidence! But no matter how close the resemblance was, it couldn't be me. I'm up in space! So it's no surprise that this person didn't turn around at first when Randy repeatedly shouted my name, then they seemed to recognize him and then quickly ran away looking panicky. Old Randy probably spooked them. He's pretty weird looking. But I can promise him that it wasn't me! I'm preparing to be the first person ever to step foot on the surface of the moon. That's about as far away from the Stop 'N' Shop as possible. And even if it was me (which it wasn't) why would I be wearing a false beard? It just sounds crazy. I'm an astronaut!

It was so sweet that you called my house to leave a message for me to hear on my safe return. You guys really are the best. No, I've no idea who it was that answered the phone. And I don't really have an explanation for them saying 'Hello Commander Neil Armstrong speaking'. I think Janet's having some work done on the kitchen while I'm away, so it may have been a workman having a joke at your expense. Which may explain why they adopted a French accent, shouted a number of profanities and then put the phone down so quickly. I'll try to find out if Janet knows anything about it, but there's not too much I can do. I'm up here in space!

To answer little Jimmy's question, yes we do have ice cream up here, but it comes in a tube like toothpaste! And no, I don't know why he thought he saw a boom mike in the shot when they showed mission footage on the news. No boom mikes up here in space! Just stars, rocks and the eternity of the universe. It may have been a shadow caused by Buzz's space suit. They are quite bulky. Need a lot of protection when you're up in space!

And thank Auntie Jeannie for her kind words. I don't really know what she means by 'Give my regards to Stanley Kubrick'. Does she mean my neighbor? His name is Stanley Kranston. And anyway, I'm not likely to see him, I'm up in space! I really am up in space.

OK, better sign off. It can get quite exhausting floating about in zero gravity, preparing the lunar rover, making sure the equipment is tested and getting geared up for the historic moment when I step foot on the surface of the moon. Up here. In space.

God Bless America,

Neil

P.S. I know the postmark may say 'Studio City, Burbank', that's just where the NASA guys send the post from. I'm in space!

To answer little Jimmy's question, yes we do have ice cream up here, but it comes in a tube like toothpaste! And no, I don't know why he thought he saw a boom mike in the shot when they showed mission footage on the news. No boom mikes up here in space! Just stars, rocks and the eternity of the universe. It may have been a shadow caused by Buzz's space suit. They are quite bulky. Need a lot of protection when you're up in space!

And thank Auntie Jeannie for her kind words. I don't really know what she means by 'Give my regards to Stanley Kubrick'. Does she mean my neighbor? His name is Stanley Kranston. And anyway, I'm not likely to see him, I'm up in space! I really am up in space.

OK, better sign off. It can get quite exhausting floating about in zero gravity, preparing the lunar rover, making sure the equipment is tested and getting geared up for the historic moment when I step foot on the surface of the moon. Up here. In space.

God Bless America,
Neil

P.S. I know the postmark may say 'Studio City, Burbank', that's just where the NASA guys send the post from. I'm in space!

FROM THE

Family Buck

MISSOULA, MONTANA

13th November 1922

Dear Sir,

My wife and I had the deep misfortune of dining at your establishment during a recent visit to New York City. Though the food was
perfectly serviceable and the surroundings splendid, I was amazed by the
quality of fellow patrons allowed onto the premises.

We were seated in the Pergola Room and almost instantly some barbed
remarks were made about my wife's choice of hat from the large group of
people at the next table. A female member of the party, who I later discovered is some sort of writer or other, claimed the hat resembled a horse's
abortion. I found this remark tasteless and unpleasant, but it appeared to
spur on her rowdy and ridiculous compatriots. A larger gentleman in
glasses then claimed that rather than a 'horse's abortion' the hat looked
like a 'turd in the Pope's swimming pool'.

Firstly, despite the laughter this remark provoked, this comment
makes no sense at all. And secondly, as a Catholic, I found it to be incredibly upsetting. I attempted to keep my resolve and ignore the rabble but
this seemed only to agitate them further. The 'horse abortion' woman
attempted to gain my attention by yelling the phrase 'Hey dick cheese' in
my direction for a matter of minutes. I'll note that at this point your wait
staff were nowhere to be found.

By now my wife was on the verge of tears. This appeared to be blood in
the water for this particular group of sharks. Sensing her distress, a
number of the men in the group began to chant 'horse abortion blub
blub' while the bespectacled man invented a vulgar, satirical musical
number concerning the size, shape and, I'm afraid, smell of my wife's hind
portions. His singing was both loud and out of tune.

I could take this provocation no further and offered any members of
the party to join me outside where we would settle the dispute in a manner

FROM THE

Family Buck

MISSOULA, MONTANA

befitting gentlemen. This prompted one of them, who may even have been a homosexual man, to perform what only can be described as an offensive series of dance moves, his gyrations rhythmically punctuated by raspberry blowing.

By now our appetizers had arrived and my wife was inconsolable. I went off to seek the manager but I was told he had 'gone to lunch'. We then left immediately without payment. Our departure was met by these louts emitting remarks of a nature too disgusting to report in full, but they continued to concern the nature of my wife's anatomy, the appearance of her hat and, again, the dick cheese thing.

The rest of our day was obviously ruined. We had plans to visit Central Park and possibly see the revue 'The Bombshells of Broadway' but we were too unsettled. My wife is still weeping and she has burnt the much-mocked headgear. I enclose a bill for a replacement of this item and demand an apology at the very least.

I will add that this trip was our anniversary celebration, but from now on will surely be remembered as the horse abortion vacation. I am a highly regarded dentist in my hometown of Missoula, Montana and write a column on vegetable growth in my local newspaper so, obviously, I am used to more respect than the amount displayed to me in your hotel.

I thought the Algonquin was a sophisticated establishment. However, you should seriously consider the disquieting elements you allow to frequent your dining hall or your fate will surely be sealed in a negative fashion. I take solace in knowing my own personal accomplishments will be remembered far longer than the distasteful bellowings of this ill-mannered group.

Yours angrily,

INFORMATION TO ALL PIZZA ARCHIPELAGO EMPLOYEES ON THE ARRIVAL OF VAN MORRISON

Dear Customer Care Operatives,

As you may be aware, a concert is taking place at the McKinley County Fairgrounds this Sunday with THE LEGENDARY VAN MORRISON™ scheduled to perform. We have been notified by THE LEGENDARY VAN MORRISON™'s management that the gentleman in question may bestow upon us the honor of visiting our particular Pizza Archipelago prior to performance. If this situation does occur, they have provided the following set of rules and stipulations concerning the visit:

1. THE LEGENDARY VAN MORRISON™ should always be referred to as THE LEGENDARY VAN MORRISON™ in both print and speech. For instance, a server should say, 'More Ice Tea, THE LEGENDARY VAN MORRISON™?' Try to get across that you are using capital letters when uttering his name.

2. All operatives should be at a 45 degree angle facing away from THE LEGENDARY VAN MORRISON™ at all times. If THE LEGENDARY VAN MORRISON™ should turn in any direction, the server should compensate accordingly, ensuring the correct angle is always maintained. THE LEGENDARY VAN MORRISON™ will have devices on hand to check this. It is worth practicing your technique on colleagues prior to the visit.

3. THE LEGENDARY VAN MORRISON™ will not eat or recognize anything colored white. If any white foodstuff is presented before him or any of his party, instant termination will occur. This applies specifically to cauliflower cheese.

4. Ensure that a distance of at least nine inches is left between you and THE LEGENDARY VAN MORRISON™. Never touch him, his clothing, his cape, his cane, his hat, the hockey stick he likes to carry or any of his bangles. Human hands must never touch his food, cutlery or crockery at any time. A set of sterilized tongs and an instructional DVD on their use will be shipped to the facility prior to the visit.

Pizza Archipelago

Head Office
29.10.11

Dear Customer Care Operatives,

As you may be aware, a concert is taking place at the McKinley County Fairgrounds this Sunday with THE LEGENDARY VAN MORRISON™ scheduled to perform. We have been notified by THE LEGENDARY VAN MORRISON™'s management that the gentleman in question may bestow upon us the honour of visiting our particular Pizza Archipelago prior to performance. If this situation does occur, they have provided the following set of rules and stipulations concerning the visit:

1. THE LEGENDARY VAN MORRISON™ should always be referred to as THE LEGENDARY VAN MORRISON™ in both print and speech. For instance, a server should say, 'More Ice Tea, THE LEGENDARY VAN MORRISON™?' Try to get across that you are using capital letters when uttering his name.

2. All operatives should be at a 45 degree angle facing away from THE LEGENDARY VAN MORRISON™ at all times. If THE LEGENDARY VAN MORRISON™ should turn in any direction, the server should compensate accordingly, ensuring the correct angle is always maintained. THE LEGENDARY VAN MORRISON™ will have devices on hand to check this. It is worth practicing your technique on colleagues prior to the visit.

3. THE LEGENDARY VAN MORRISON™ will not eat or recognize anything coloured white. If any white foodstuff is presented before him or any of his party, instant termination will occur. This applies specifically to cauliflower cheese.

4. Ensure that a distance of at least nine inches is left between you and THE LEGENDARY VAN MORRISON™. Never touch him, his clothing, his cape, his cane, his hat, the hockey stick he likes to carry or any of his bangles. Human hands must never touch his food, cutlery or crockery at any time. A set of sterilized tongs and an instructional DVD on their use will be shipped to the facility prior to the visit.

45° angle

9" distance

5. THE LEGENDARY VAN MORRISON™ will almost certainly not communicate with you in any way, but on occasion he has been known to comment in a derogatory fashion to the people around him. His accent and cadence can be quite hard to understand, but if you feel him suddenly staring at you making a noise similar to 'MNWAH!' 'MNWAH!' then he is making a joke at your expense. Laugh vigorously if this should happen. Roll around on the floor clutching your sides, if this is feasible. It may appear sarcastic, but THE LEGENDARY VAN MORRISON™ is unable to detect sarcasm due to his Irish upbringing.

6. Those in THE LEGENDARY VAN MORRISON™ party may be quivering or lightly sobbing. Don't draw attention to this.

7. Obviously the restaurant will be closed to all other patrons. A single family of four will be present throughout the meal to add a semblance of normality to the proceedings and for THE LEGENDARY VAN MORRISON™ to have something to throw his breadsticks at. This family will be provided by us.

8. THE LEGENDARY VAN MORRISON™ will demand food that is the polar opposite of the food you actually serve. If possible, try to imagine what that food could be and make sure you have the relevant ingredients in stock. Though in our experience this is usually impossible to gauge.

9. Those attending to THE LEGENDARY VAN MORRISON™ should have an obvious physical defect or deformity to put him at ease. This can take the form of an eye-patch, mono-brow, facial scar, blackened teeth, head lump or missing limb. Obviously fake versions of these are perfectly acceptable as THE LEGENDARY VAN MORRISON™ doesn't seem to recognize the difference.

10. At the conclusion of the meal, THE LEGENDARY VAN MORRISON™ will not expect to pay and in fact the server will be expected to offer him money and jewels to recognize the honor of being in his company. All such payments, and any damages incurred as THE LEGENDARY VAN MORRISON™ leaves the location, will be fully reimbursed.

Adhere to these few simple requests and together we can ensure THE LEGENDARY VAN MORRISON™'s visit to your establishment will not become a harrowing ordeal. Photographic opportunities and complementary tickets to the concert will obviously not be available.

5. THE LEGENDARY VAN MORRISON™ will almost certainly not communicate with you in any way, but on occasion he has been known to comment in a derogatory fashion to the people around him. His accent and cadence can be quite hard to understand, but if you feel him suddenly staring at you making a noise similar to 'MNWAH!' 'MNWAH!' then he is making a joke at your expense. Laugh vigorously if this should happen. Roll around on the floor clutching your sides, if this is feasible. It may appear sarcastic, but THE LEGENDARY VAN MORRISON™ is unable to detect sarcasm due to his Irish upbringing.

6. Those in THE LEGENDARY VAN MORRISON™ party may be quivering or lightly sobbing. Don't draw attention to this.

7. Obviously the restaurant will be closed to all other patrons. A single family of four will be present throughout the meal to add a semblance of normality to the proceedings and for THE LEGENDARY VAN MORRISON™ to have something to throw his breadsticks at. This family will be provided by us.

8. THE LEGENDARY VAN MORRISON™ will demand food that is the polar opposite of the food you actually serve. If possible, try to imagine what that food could be and make sure you have the relevant ingredients in stock. Though in our experience this is usually impossible to gauge.

9. Those attending to THE LEGENDARY VAN MORRISON™ should have an obvious physical defect or deformity to put him at ease. This can take the form of an eye-patch, mono-brow, facial scar, blackened teeth, head lump or missing limb. Obviously fake versions of these are perfectly acceptable as THE LEGENDARY VAN MORRISON™ doesn't seem to recognize the difference.

10. At the conclusion of the meal, THE LEGENDARY VAN MORRISON™ will not expect to pay and in fact the server will be expected to offer him money and jewels to recognize the honor of being in his company. All such payments, and any damages incurred as THE LEGENDARY VAN MORRISON™ leaves the location, will be fully reimbursed.

Adhere to these few simple requests and together we can ensure THE LEGENDARY VAN MORRISON™'s visit to your establishment will not become a harrowing ordeal. Photographic opportunities and complimentary tickets to the concert will obviously not be available.

You enter from the side. There is a road ahead of you. The road is straight like a lie is straight. There is a KFC on the right hand side. One of those combo ones with a Taco Bell inside. The sign is bleached and cracked where the sun has eaten at it. You may as well ignore this. If you can.

Then you will keep going straight. The smell of burning wood will grow distracting. It's from Smokies Original Wood Fired Pizza. Their doughballs are excellent. I once found some hair in my Caesar salad. I can never go there again. Dogs are not allowed.

The road continues past thick houses contained by white wooden fences. You can never know what is going on behind them. But you can imagine. There is a store selling sewing machines. There seems to be no place to turn. Then there is a place to turn. You turn. Left.

The road is lined with trees now. It shakes something inside of you. Were you once in these very woods alone? Were you cold and tired in there, huddled against a rock? Did I miss the sign I was looking out for when I was thinking about this? No, you have many more miles to go. You haven't even reached the Outback Steakhouse.

You reach the Outback Steakhouse. A taste of copper fills your mouth. There is a stop sign then a stoplight and then a stop sign. You need to pee. You are out of Cheetos. Is it safe to continue this way? Do you stop at the Conoco? You quickly make a rudimentary calculation in your mind. The hunger gnaws away. The pressure that is applied to the bladder. The degree of desire for a Mounds bar and a Diet Sprite. You pull over. Sitting in the gloom, waiting for a sign, waiting for inspiration to fall. Nothing. You proceed.

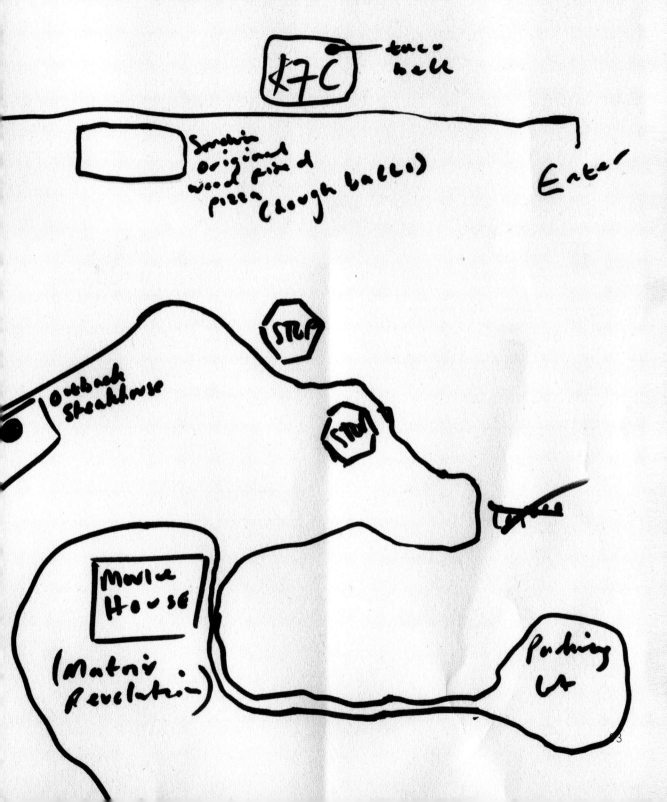

You turn on the wipers. You don't know why. Just their sound is a kind of music. There is a sign for a rest stop. You can picture a wire rack inside. The Best of Loggins and Messina. $1.99. A gumball machine. The smell of urinal cakes. Lust.

You pass a Chevy. And a Lexus. And a Volvo. You drive into a storm. The rain hits the window hard and makes a sound like clapping. A movie house. It is showing *The Matrix Revolutions*. You wonder why. You try to remember if that's the one with the weird rave. And all the mud people. It's good to remember. It's also good to pay attention to road signs. You've missed your turn.

You will be forced to pull a U-turn. A strip mall parking lot. An asshole in a Nissan Cherry cuts you up, eager for a parking space. You give him the finger. It is the wrong finger. You feel like a fool. You take this anger back onto the road. The movie house looms again. *Matrix Revolutions*. You make the turn.

Darkness falls like a big kitten. A cold, autistic, stupid, stinky dark. You really need to pee now. You look around the vehicle. There is an empty can. Pepsi Max. You could pee in that. Angle your dick hole over the can's mouth. But what if it fills? Overflows. Hot, frothy piss dripping onto your lap and fingers. What if you catch your Jap's Eye on the sharp metallic edge? You wince at the thought. You hold on. The fat moon rises in a gap. Between mountains. A sign tells you there are no rest stops on this road. You have far to go.

WILBUR WRIGHT WRITES TO HIS BROTHER

Wilbur Wright

ENQUIRY NUMBER — Established 1892
INSTITUTION DEPARTMENT — RECEIVED APP2039
FOR TO

ANS'D

DAYTON, OHIO. 16th December 1903

Orville,

    The great day is almost upon us. The day where our achievements will alter the history of mankind and finally confirm that human beings are capable of mechanical flight.

    Once the wheels of our aeronautical craft are unbounded from the earth and rise into the sky, fulfilling the manifest dreams of generations, our names will surely be cemented into legend.

    And it is because I have such massive respect for you, my dear brother, and consider you the impetus and the heart and soul of this entire project that I insist you go first.

    Now, I don't want any arguments about this, Orville. We both know that thanks to our endeavors and our meticulous testing, the craft is almost certainly safe and will surely become airborne without any problems or perceived tragic, fiery accidents. I am so certain of our skills in this area (particularly your efforts, sweet Orville) that I feel confident in my insistence that you attempt the first experimental manned flight.

    Once your own heroic pursuits have been confirmed and you land safely (as we both know you almost certainly will), I will be honored to enter the aircraft and attempt the second flight. While I hope we shall both be equally recognized for this achievement, I would be more than happy for you to take all the accolades, in the same way that if (and we both know this won't happen) some disaster should occur (and it won't), I will be more than happy to honor your memory in the appropriate fashion. But, of course, that is impossible, you will excel and it will be a relief to me, knowing you flew and survived and I was worthy enough to shadow your remarkable conduct.

    I shall meet you at the airfield as planned, dear brother, where I really, really hope you will be the first man to undertake flight.

Your brother, Wilbur

    P.S. I think I may also suffer from vertigo all of a sudden so, again, perhaps it is best that you go first.

Letters of Not No. 27

```
DAVID SIMON
WRITES TO
HBO INC
```

Dear Cliff,

Thanks for inviting me along to provide commentary for the forthcoming Special Edition Boxset of *The Complete Wire*. I'm afraid I will have to decline at this time.

Problem is, I'm still working my way through it. I started re-watching the whole thing, but I got sort of stuck in the middle of Season 3. Don't get me wrong, I'm really enjoying it. Addictive stuff. But then I planned to watch it on vacation and I brought along the wrong disc by mistake, then I started watching *The West Wing* instead and really got into that and there are like fifteen seasons of it or something, then I tried to find the disc for *The Wire* and I'd left it on top of the DVD player and it got all dusty and I tried to clean it and I think I scratched it because it looked all weird, so I'll need to get another one eventually and I couldn't really keep track of what was going on. They appeared to be talking about hamsters, which just confused me. But I'm definitely going to go back and finish it.

But until I do that, I probably shouldn't commentate. Why not get the guy who played Omar to take part? Or does he die at the start? I honestly can't remember. There are so many characters, it's hard to keep track.

Best,
David

DAVID SIMON

Dear Cliff,

Thanks for inviting me along to provide commentary for the forthcoming Special Edition Boxset of 'The Complete Wire'. I'm afraid I will have to decline at this time.

Problem is, I'm still working my way through it. I started re-watching the whole thing, but I got sort of stuck in the middle of Season 3. Don't get me wrong, I'm really enjoying it. Addictive stuff. But then I planned to watch it on vacation and I brought along the wrong disc by mistake, then I started watching *The West Wing* instead and really got into that and there are like fifteen seasons of it or something, then I tried to find the disc for *The Wire* and I'd left it on top of the DVD player and it got all dusty and I tried to clean it and I think I scratched it because it looked all weird, so I'll need to get another one eventually and I couldn't really keep track of what was going on. They appeared to be talking about hamsters, which just confused me. But I'm definitely going to go back and finish it.

But until I do that, I probably shouldn't commentate. Why not get the guy who played Omar to take part? Or does he die at the start? I honestly can't remember. There are so many characters, it's hard to keep track.

Best,

David

12th March 1860

Dear Mr Krugerschmidt,

As you are aware, I allowed my agents here in England to deal with the American publication of my work *On the Origin of Species*. Due to my pressing work schedule, I had no involvement in the venture whatsoever and assumed that this would be merely be a straightforward reproduction of the British edition.

So, it was with a certain amount of alarm that I received your letter dated March 9th concerning future versions of the work. When you suggest I write a second volume entitled *Uh Oh, Even More Origins of Species* to be followed by another called *Good Gravy, Yet More Origins of Species* I got the distinct impression you may not be treating my research and findings with the seriousness indentured within it.

With trepidation, I sought out the American edition of my work as published by your company 'Krugerschmidt Laugh Factory Publications'. I was further alarmed to see the lettering used on the cover was in a font I believe is known as 'Comic Sans' and featured, at my initial inspection, nine exclamation marks of differing sizes. I'd like to point out that the British edition of the *Origin of Species* featured no exclamation marks whatsoever.

But this was nothing compared to the illustration adorning the exterior that appeared to show a caricature of someone, who I can only assume to be myself, naked, hairy, ape-like and apparently engaged in throwing a collection of my own faeces towards the direction of the reader. On the reverse side I discovered the following synopsis: 'Hang onto your pith helmets as old Professor Yuk Yuks takes you on the wackiest, hackiest, cracking up-iest adventure this side of the ape house. You'll be shouting "nuts to you!" as he tells us that we're all monkey men. Hey, guess that's why I love bananas! You banana!'

12 March 1860

Dear Mr Brongersholdt

If you are aware I allowed my agents here in
England to deal with the American publication of
my work the Origin of Species due to my
pressing work schedule I had no involvement in the
various whatsoever and assumed that they would be
merely be a straightforward reproduction of the
British edition

So it is with a certain amount of alarm that I
received your letters dated March 9th concerning
future copying of the work when you suggest
Origins of Species to be followed by another called
God Swung Yet More Origins of Species I get the
distinct impression you may not be tracking my
approach and findings with the principles
indoctrinated within it

With trepidation I sought out the American edition
of my work as published by your company
Brongersholdt Laugh Tielberg Publications I was further
alarmed to see the lettering used on the cover my in
a font I believe is known as Comic Sans and featured
at my critical junctures more exclamation marks of
of differing sizes I'd like to point out that the
the British edition of the Origin of Species featured
no exclamation marks whatsoever

nothing compared to the illustration
99

...the direction of the reader on the voyage, John

...discovered the following synopsis; they make your path
blatantly as old Professor told Jolly (okay you on the evening
burlesque cracking synopsis elevation they joke of the age
keep youth be flooding only to you up his folly up that
...all wending ... they guess that's why I have
...becomes? You know...

...I constructed a bridge/house on the ... of New
...and was informed that my book would be found in
...in the ... portion of that particular store. What
I mean the gentleman then approved me it was selling
like hot cakes, and a real treat. Now I am not sure what
my ... informed you prior to the publication of my
work but let me state unequivocally that they write as
an important scientific research document and not
...not a mere frippery for the amusement of...

...I'm afraid these future ... you synopses will not
be forthcoming from me however. Should you wish to
find another author to produce these materials perhaps
... can work out some sort of licensing deal. Science
may be important but there's no money in it.
My people will be in touch with your people.

Yours,

    Charles Darwin

P.S. Also your last royalty payment reached me four
days later than ...

On a hunch, I contacted a bookseller in the city of New York and was informed that my book could be found in the 'Humour' section of that particular store. What is more the gentleman then assured me it was 'selling like hot cakes' and 'a real hoot'. Now, I am not sure what my agents informed you prior to the publication of my work, but let me state unequivocally that this work is an important scientific research document and not a mere frippery for the amusement of Americans.

So, I'm afraid these future editions you propose will not be forthcoming from me. However, should you wish to find another author to produce this material, perhaps we can work out some sort of licensing deal. Science may be important, but there's no money in it. My people will be in touch with your people.

Yours,
Charles Darwin

P.S. Also, your last royalty payment reached me four days later than promised. Please ensure these are made on time in future.

WHEN CALIGULA BECAME EMPEROR, HE MADE A LOT OF PROMISES TO ORDINARY ROMANS LIKE YOU. BUT HAS HE MADE GOOD ON THOSE PROMISES?

CALIGULA PROMISED US A RAISE IN PAY AND MORE SESTERTII IN OUR POCKETS. BUT INSTEAD HE PROMOTED HIS HORSE TO HIGH ELECTORAL OFFICE.

CALIGULA ASSERTED THAT THE INVASION AND DEFEAT OF BRITANNIA WAS IMMINENT, BRINGING FURTHER GLORY TO THE EMPIRE. INSTEAD, HE FORCED THE NAVY TO WAGE WAR AGAINST NEPTUNE, ATTACK THE SEA AND TAKE SHELLS AS 'SPOILS'.

CALIGULA CLAIMED THERE WOULD BE NEW AQUEDUCTS BRINGING FRESH WATER INTO THE CITY OF ROME. INSTEAD, HE SEDUCED AND PENETRATED VAST NUMBERS OF PEOPLE INCLUDING VARIOUS FAMILY MEMBERS AND A SELECTION OF RANDOM PASSING ANIMALS.

CALIGULA SAID THE PRICE OF GRAIN WOULD BE SLASHED INSTEAD, HE FED LOTS OF PEOPLE TO LIONS FOR HIS OWN AMUSEMENT AND FREQUENTLY STABBED HOUSEGUESTS 'FOR A LAUGH'.

CALIGULA PROMISED TO SORT OUT THE POTHOLES THAT ARE CURRENTLY PLAGUING THE VIA APPIA. INSTEAD, HE DECLARED HIMSELF A GOD AND ORDERED THE POPULATION TO WORSHIP HIM WHILE ERECTING ENORMOUS STATUES OF HIMSELF IN TEMPLES ACROSS THE CITY AND THEN STABBING THE STATUES.

DON'T YOU THINK IT'S TIME FOR A CHANGE?

When Caligula became Emperor, he made a lot of promises to ordinary Romans like you. But has he made good on those promises?

Caligula promised us a raise in pay and more sestertii in our pockets. But instead he promoted his horse to high electoral office.

Caligula asserted that the invasion and defeat of Britannia was imminent, bringing further glory to the Empire. Instead, he forced the navy to wage war against Neptune, attack the sea and take shells as 'spoils'.

Caligula claimed there would be new aqueducts bringing fresh water into the city of Rome. Instead, he seduced and penetrated vast numbers of people including various family members and a selection of random passing animals.

Caligula said the price of grain would be slashed. Instead, he fed lots of people to lions for his own amusement and frequently stabbed houseguests 'for a laugh'.

Caligula promised to sort out the potholes that are currently plaguing the Via Appia. Instead, he declared himself a god and ordered the population to worship him while erecting enormous statues of himself in temples across the city and then stabbing the statues.

Don't you think it's time for a change?

Have you thought about Claudius lately? Yes he has a limp, a stutter and possible epilepsy and is considered a farting, bumbling laughing stock throughout the Empire, BUT:

FACT! Claudius has a real understanding of complicated infrastructure problems and has never intended to install any of his farm animals to high political positions.

FACT! Claudius has a three-pronged plan to defeat Britannia and realises that doing battle with gods such as Neptune and stealing their shells is not a reliable foreign policy standpoint.

FACT! Claudius realises the desire for fresh water and the vital need for drainage change, while never intending to sleep with any close family members.

FACT! Claudius has a plan to import cheap grain from Egypt, which will vastly reduce prices and he has only ever stabbed anyone repeatedly for either sport or in self-defence.

FACT! Claudius is just as annoyed with the pothole problem as anyone in Rome and he does not envisage a time when he will insist on being considered a god.

If you want clean water, cheap grain, less incest, reduced random stabbings, a more cohesive foreign policy, better schools and fewer equine politicians, perhaps it's time to think about Claudius.

CLAUDIUS – THE FAIRLY SANE CHOICE

[Paid for by the campaign to repeatedly stab Caligula and throw him in a lake]

AUDIO GUIDE TO RIPON CATHEDRAL

Please press button one

Enter by the eastern narthex. Beware the frantic verger.
Look at the transepts! Look at the transepts! Much bigger
than a Lambretta. Bitter in their stony standing.

Glass stained with middle-class pebble dash. As Mr Fryer
takes a pew. Mr Fryer? Mr Fryer? Him with the bent up
wife? 'Have you seen his leather sofa?' Yes! He looks upon
the clerestory with glowing greed. He takes in the rotunda **YES!**
like white sliced. Pass by him, stay straight on this path
and hope.

Please press button two

Don't look at the lectern! Don't look at the lectern! The
Choirmaster only has one eye. And the other is milky like
ponds. The crypt is closed for cleaning. E.G. Bypass and
try the colonnade. It was built by a man in a century. I
am a gothic magistrate. You are the Pope of brass. It is
too late to get your money back.

Dead souls under your loafers. Look at their dark names
on the stones. Don't mither them, they have no lungs.
The font was forged by blasted hands. Jimmy, wet the
baby's head in there and notably at the Cathedral of the
Dormition at Smolensk. How can you stand here now when
Blockbusters is on? Shuffle up to the pulpit. Ginger! A
tapestry!

Please press button three

In Ripon. In Ely. In Bury. In Londis. In Hitler's bunker
with his limp. All will be built out of blocks. How dare
you say this is revivalist. Can't you hear the organ's
monkey? His fat fingers hit the pipes like flared corn. He
has seen the misericord. Have you seen the misericord?
Enter the apse! Enter the apse! Dusty in here and there
are no toilets. E.S.P. You can see how I feel about the
bema. There are four corners on this tour. You will see
none of them. **NONE**

Here comes the irate precentor. He has a corrected
posture. Utterly Butterly! Utterly Butterly! There is
a chalice in a glass case. The sign reads, don't touch
the glass case. Elastic bands hold the anger in place.
Head forward!

DON'T!

A velvet rope prevents your access. You cannot go
behind the scenes. Scenes are stains on unfashionable
jeans. Did I mention the stained glass windows? Ah
yes, I see that I did earlier. Turn left and pace to
the void.

Please press button four

Press button four now! Press button four now! You are
in the outside, outside! Belligerent gargoyles cling
to the guttering. Garry Bushell in grey stone. Their
parkas are all ill-fitting. There once was a vane up
there. It was secreted by a sad slim Santa.

Turn west now and walk abruptly. Time for tea with all
that cadence. Dapper Dan the dandy lout. He is provost
of the snack bar. Twix and Fanta for two pound twenty.
£2.20
Crumbed sugar blights formica. Sit by a small school
party. They're excited by the key rings.

There is nothing left. There is nothing left. Just
glance at the sickly postcards. Gathered on their
rack like crucified spines. An old man weeps on his
bony seat as you throw a penny in the charity circus.
Press button four now! There is no God. Exit via
the draughty atrium. Outside! It will probably be
mistling. Time to pull your hoodie's cord. The sky
dripping wet like pies.

NOTHING

JANE AUSTEN WRITES TO A LOVE RIVAL

14th August 1797

My dear Miss Hollis,

It was such a delight to see you at the Ashe Ball this last Saturday eve. I had heard much of your beauty and wit but none of the reports contrived to offer you enough flattery.

It was a delight to see you in the same room as Mr Thomas LeForge, a gentleman whose acquaintance I have made often. Which brings me to the purpose of this letter. I feel I must confide in you concerning a certain disturbance I felt in regards to yourself and the previously mentioned Mr LeForge. Mr LeForge is a dear, dear friend of mine and we have attended many of the same balls. We have often stared across the room and sat together. Strictly in that order, Miss Hollis. Only I could not help but observe that you were witnessed staring across the room at him. And I can only assume that your thoughts would have eventually drifted towards a seat with him.

I think it is quite understandable that any lady would be delighted to make the acquaintance of Mr LeForge due to the eloquence of his wit and the power of his lower limbs, which are lithe and flexible from grouse hunting. And certainly you would not be the first lady in the district to stare across the room at him. His visage is adequately populated. However, I cannot countenance as to why you would ever even dream of sitting with Mr LeForge for any portion of the evening.

As you were well aware, I am known for my sitting with Mr LeForge and have sat with him, at balls, on many previous occasions. I would go as far to say that I have often very forcefully sat with Mr LeForge, using my full body weight to sink aggressively into the chair. There have even been moments when our legs would lightly brush against each other during the course of our forceful and expressive sitting. Obviously on these occasions, apologies were profusely offered, all parties immediately leaving the venue and no mentions of it were ever made again for fear of the scandal that would surely erupt.

14th August
1797

My dear Miss Hollis,

It was such a delight to see you at the Ashe Ball this last Saturday eve. I had heard much of your beauty and wit but none of the reports contrived to offer you enough flattery.

It was a delight to see you in the same room as Mr Eoin LeForge, a gentleman whose acquaintance I have made often. Which brings me to the purpose of this letter. I feel I must confide in you concerning a certain disturbance I felt in regards to yourself and the previously mentioned Mr LeForge. Mr LeForge is a dear, dear friend of mine and we have attended many of the same balls. We have often stared across the room and sat together. ~~Strictly~~ in that order Miss Hollis. Only I could not help but observe that you were witnessed stari~~ng~~ across the room at him. And I can only assume that your thoughts would have eventually drifted towards a seat with him.

I think it is quite understandable that any lady would be delighted to make the acquaintance of Mr LeForge due to the eloquence of his wit and the power of his lower limbs, which are lithe and flexible from ~~our~~ hunting. And certainly you would not be the first lady in the ~~dis~~trict to stare across the room at him. His visage is adequately ~~mod~~ulated. However, I cannot coun~~tenance~~ as to why you would ever even dream of sitting with Mr LeForge for any portion of the evening.

As you were well aware, I am known for my sitting with Mr LeForge and have sat with him, at balls, on many previous occasions. I would go as far to say that I have often very force~~ful~~ly sat with Mr LeForge, using my full body weight to sink aggressi~~vely~~ into the chair. There have even been moments when our legs would lightly brush against each other during the course of our forceful and expressive sitting. Obviously on these occasions, apologies were profusely offered, all parties immediately leaving the venue and no mentions of it were ever made again for fear of the scandal that would surely erupt.

This sitting only came after an extended peri~~od~~ of staring across the room. I would say that the staring across the room component lasted at least six mont~~hs~~ before any sitting was even considered. It now seems there is a danger of young ladies leaping into the sitting position after only a quick glance or two. It's *simply not* how things are done.

That is the extent of our sitting Miss Hollis, so I think you can understand my abject ~~horror~~ terror to see you staring at the gentleman in question, with sitting on your mind. From what I have heard, Mr LeForge would not be the first gentleman you have considered sitting with. I have it on good authority that you have previously sat with a whole host of gentlemen including Lord Barrington, Mr Grantington, Mr Hardacre, Viceroy Chapps and the Right Reverend Samuels. Twice. I would have thought you would have been quite tired and sore after so much unbridled sitting activity. And yet you still found the energy to stare towards my dear friend Mr LeForge. Quite a testament to your *reserves of energy*.

You are quite new to our little community Miss Hollis and perhaps in your previous circle of friends such abundant staring and sitting with random gentlemen was acceptable. But that is not how we do things at the Grange. I will presume this was a mere misunderstanding and there will not be a repeat of this staring and prospective sitting in the future. Otherwise, I can assure you that you will have considerable trouble ever sitting again.

Yours,

Miss Jane Austen

This sitting only came after an extended period of staring across the room. I would say that the staring across the room component lasted at least six months before any sitting was even considered. It now seems there is a danger of young ladies leaping into the sitting position after only a quick glance or two. It's simply not how things are done.

That is the extent of our sitting, Miss Hollis, so I think you can understand my abject horror to see you staring at the gentleman in question, with sitting on your mind. From what I have heard, Mr LeForge would not be the first gentleman you have considered sitting with. I have it on good authority that you have previously sat with a whole host of gentlemen including Lord Barrington, Mr Grantington, Mr Hardacre, Viceroy Chapps and the Right Reverend Samuels. Twice.

I would have thought you would have been quite tired and sore after so much unbridled sitting activity. And yet you still found the energy to stare towards my dear friend Mr LeForge. Quite a testament to your reserves of energy!

You are quite new to our little community, Miss Hollis, and perhaps in your previous circle of friends such abundant staring and sitting with random gentlemen was acceptable. But that is not how we do things at the Grange. I will presume this was a mere misunderstanding and there will not be a repeat of this staring and prospective sitting in the future. Otherwise, I can assure you that you will have considerable trouble ever sitting again.

Yours,
Miss Jane Austen

CAPTAIN SCOTT'S *OTHER* LAST LETTER TO HIS WIFE

March 1912

My darling dearest,

By now the missive recounting my pain at being apart from you should have arrived. The sentiments expressed therein still hold true of course. You mean more to me than anything, which I hope I made clear in the previous letter. It's just that I've remembered some other stuff, of a more practical nature, that should also be addressed.

I'm expecting delivery of a Parka jacket sometime in the next couple of weeks. Obviously. this should have arrived prior to the expedition, but the outfitters have been manifest in their buffoonery. I would like you to return this item, demanding a full refund and expressly pointing out their lack of commercial responsibility. And please make clear my personal indignation (feel free to show them this letter if necessary). If they continue to give you grief (as is their wont, let me tell you, especially an older gentleman called Standing whose dedication to officiousness is as committed as mine to Polar expedition) perhaps include a few cuttings regarding the tragic nature of my fate (should this occur, fingers crossed and all that).

While on the subject of blaggards, be wary of that fellow who washes the windows. He's always trying to increase his prices and then saying things like: 'Oh, Mr Scott said it would be all right, before he went off to the North Pole.' He does the windows of quite a few of the explorers and he's tried it on with all of them. He seems to focus on the ones not likely to return, that's his angle. He charges Shackleton £4 a year! He's only got a bungalow. Really quite ridiculous.

Also, me and the lads were just having a bit of a chat in the tent and it was imparted to me that I do sometimes come across as a bit of a fuddy-duddy. Perhaps, when speaking of me to the press (should the inevitable occur), you could highlight my more playful side? I don't wish to go down in history as a big grump. Make me appear less dour. 'As my husband always used to quip, "no-one likes the cold shoulder!"' Not that exactly, but like that.

March 1912

My darling dearest,

By now the missive recounting my pain at being apart from you should have arrived. The sentiments expressed therein still hold true of course. You mean more to me than anything, which I hope I made clear in the previous letter. It's just that I've remembered some other stuff, of a more practical nature, that should also be addressed.

I'm expecting delivery of a Parka jacket sometime in the next couple of weeks. Obviously, this should have arrived prior to the expedition, but the outfitters have been manifest in their buffoonery. I would like you to return this item, demanding a full refund and expressly pointing out their lack of commercial responsibility. And please make clear my personal indignation (feel free to show them this letter if necessary). If they continue to give you grief (as is their wont, let me tell you, especially an older gentleman called Standing whose dedication to officiousness is as committed as mine to Polar expedition) perhaps include a few cuttings regarding the tragic nature of my fate (should this occur, fingers crossed and all that).

While on the subject of blaggards, be wary of that fellow who washes the windows. He's always trying to increase his prices and then saying things like: 'Oh, Mr Scott said it would be all right, before he went off to the North Pole'. He does the windows of quite a few of the explorers and he's tried it on with all of them. He seems to focus on the ones not likely to return, that's his angle. He charges

113

Shackleton £4 a year! He's only got a bungalow. Really quite ridiculous.

Also, me and the lads were just having a bit of a chat in the tent and it was imparted to me that I do sometimes come across as a bit of a fuddy-duddy. Perhaps, when speaking of me to the press (should the inevitable occur), you could highlight my more playful side? I don't wish to go down in history as a big grump. Make me appear less dour. 'As my husband always used to quip, "no-one likes the cold shoulder!"' Not that exactly, but like that.

Think that's everything. As you know the dog gets that worm thing sometimes, but there's little that can be done. Erm ... dum, de, dum ... oh, cancel the hall for the celebration party obviously. There's quite a bit of bunting in the loft, picked up a job lot before I left; dispose of it as you see fit (or hang onto it if you think your next husband may also be an explorer. Though I wouldn't recommend it! You see, that's the playful side I was referring to earlier).

So, I shall offer you my sweetest farewell my dearest darling, with all the love that I possess in ... oh, another thing about the Parka people, they'll claim I didn't pay a deposit (that's the sort of swines you're dealing with). There is a receipt in the bureau drawer — threaten legal action if necessary.

I really am most peeved about this.

Yours,
Scott

P.S. My love to the children etc.

Think that's everything. As you know, the dog gets that worm thing sometimes, but there's little that can be done. Erm ... dum, de, dum ... oh, cancel the hall for the celebration party obviously. There's quite a bit of bunting in the loft, picked up a job lot before I left, dispose of it as you see fit (or hang onto it, if you think your next husband may also be an explorer. Though I wouldn't recommend it! You see, that's the playful side I was referring to earlier).

So, I shall offer you my sweetest farewell my dearest darling, with all the love that I possess in ... oh, another thing about the Parka people, they'll claim I didn't pay a deposit (that's the sort of swines you're dealing with). There is a receipt in the bureau drawer – threaten legal action if necessary, I really am most peeved about this.

Yours,
Scott

P.S. Oh, love to the children etc.

AN EVICTION NOTICE FROM ST FRANCIS OF ASSISI'S LANDLORD

4th March 1220

Dear Tenant,

How many times do I have to tell you?
NO PETS. You have until the 28th to vacate the property.

Yours with regret,
Mr Prinelli

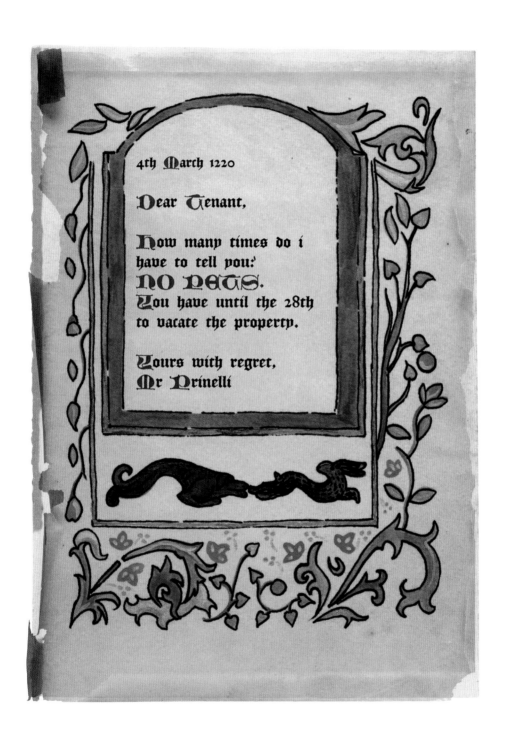

4th March 1220

Dear Tenant,

How many times do i
have to tell you:
NO PETS.
You have until the 28th
to vacate the property.

Yours with regret,
Mr Prinelli

PATTI SMITH'S
GYM APPLICATION

NAME

Call me Jimi. Call me Jagger. Call me Rimbaud. I'm every white hot bitch in heat.
I'm every black man who's ever cried. I'm a panther. A lancer. An unexplained answer.
I am New Jersey.

AGE

I slip between the Fall of Saigon and the Rise of the Transformers. Wedged beside
Burroughs in Tangiers and the space between Mickey Mouse's ears. I'm an ageless nymph,
I'm an old maid in Normandy, I'm too young to be recognized. I'm a flightless bird.

CONTACT DETAILS

Try to touch me, but you can never reach me. I'm at the Dakota. I'm in the Brady Bunch
House. I'm floating in Morrison's Paris bathtub. Look for me where I should never be,
and I have just abandoned there. You can't find me, except in the stars,
in the stars, in the stars. Infinity.

OUTSTANDING MEDICAL CONDITIONS

Veins filled with too much experience. Heart fit to burst. Hands that have felt anger
and plasticine. Eyes that have seen everything and wept often. Feet burnt black from
dancing. Asthma.

ANY SPECIAL ASSISTANCE REQUIRED

Just allow my pleasure to burst, spinning and clashing like a horse unrestrained in
a sea of piss and inevitability. Did Baudelaire need special assistance? Did Jackson
Pollock need special assistance? Did Jack Palance? Then ask them, Charlie.

GYM APPLICATION FORM

Name Call me Jimi. Call me Jagger. Call me Rimbaud. I'm every white hot bitch in heat. I'm every black man who's ever cried. I'm a panther. ~~A~~ A Cancer. An unexplained answer. I am New Jersey.

Age I slip between the fall of Saigon an the Rise of the Transformers. Wedged between Mickey Mouse's ears. I'm an ageless nymph, I'm an old maid in Normandy, I'm ~~too~~ too young to be recognised. I'm a flightless bird.

Contact Details Joy ~~To too~~ Touch me, but you can never reach me. I'm at the Dakota. I'm in the Brady Bunch House. I'm floating in Morrison's Paris bathtub. Look for me where I should never be, and I have ~~→~~ just abandoned there. You can't find me, except in the stars, in the stars, in the stars. Infinity.

Outstanding Medical Conditions Veins filled with too much experience. Heart fit to burst. Hands that have felt anger and plasticine. Eyes that have seen everything and wept often. Feet burnt black from dancing. Asthma.

Any Special Assistance Required ~~As~~ Just allow my pleasure to burst, spinning and crashing like a wave unrestrained in a sea of piss and inevitability. Did Baudelaire need special assistance? Did Jackson Pollock need special assistance? Did Jack Palance? Then ask them, Charlie.

Type Of Membership – Off Peak/Full Access If the peak can be mounted and ~~stated~~ tasted, if the angels never fell too hard to earth, littered with gems like wells of dreams. No access is ever full. Ask a Black Panther. Ask the MC5. Ask Altamont. There's always the wall of misery and calm and fog and henna.

Will You Attend Classes (I.E. Spinning/Zumba) Teachers teach the ~~truth~~ truth of lies. Switchblade kids on dark street corners know the answers. Live. Walk. Breathe. Hope. Pray. Dance. Nap. Fight. Activate. ~~Agit~~ Agitate. Eat Pizza.

Will You Require Towels Let me dry in the brittle wind ~~✗~~ of a desert storm. The sand in our faces, blazed ~~✗~~ with burning dirt. Benediction to the spirits, the lizard leading the lamb, the butcher leading the flank, the bland leading the bland.

How Did You Hear About Us Taste the word on the street. And the word is POWER. And the word is ANGER. And the word is BOXCAR. Standing on the corner, the boy ~~with~~ with the hip shake, a switchblade in your back, Jack.

Any Additional Comments

Liberté! Egalité! Cassius Clay!

TYPE OF MEMBERSHIP – OFF PEAK/FULL ACCESS

If the peak can be mounted and tasted, if the angels never fell too hard to earth, littered with gems like wells of dreams. No access is ever full. Ask a Black Panther. Ask the MC5. Ask Altamont. There's always the wall of misery and calm and fog and henna.

WILL YOU ATTEND CLASSES (i.e. SPINNING/ZUMBA)

Teachers teach the truth of lies. Switchblade kids on dark street corners know the answers. Live. Work. Breathe. Hope. Pray. Dance. Nap. Fight. Activate. Agitate. Eat pizza.

WILL YOU REQUIRE TOWELS

Let me dry in the brittle wind of a desert storm. The sand in our faces, blazed with burning dirt. Benediction to the spirits, the lizard leading the lamb, the butcher leading the flank, the bland leading the bland.

HOW DID YOU HEAR ABOUT US

Taste the word on the street. And the word is POWER. And the word is ANGER. And the word is BOXCAR. Standing on the corner, the boy with the hip shake, a switchblade in your back, Jack.

ANY ADDITIONAL COMMENTS

Liberté! Égalité! Cassius Clay!

SALVADOR DALI'S
TO DO LIST

1. Wake
2. Discard Dali's sleeping shroud
3. Wash face in the blood of a crab
4. Eat a single wren's egg
5. Shout 'Clavy, Clavy, Clavy' for no reason
6. Dali's moustache regimen
7. Dress (outrageously)
8. Call stockbroker
9. Leave dwelling
10. Buy lobster (get discount, you are Dali)
11. Buy leash (as above)
12. Startle ordinaries with lobster on leash
13. Dispose of lobster, return leash for store credit
14. Dance frenetically
15. Rest
16. Commence triptych featuring lake of oil and weird face
17. Copyright initial triptych sketches
18. Claim to be magnetic
19. Lunch. An entire roasted fawn
20. Change outfit (more outrageous)
21. Approve Dali tea-towel range
22. Appear on popular Spanish game show 'Per-Lunko'
23. Distress fellow guests with armadillo
24. Invoice for appearance on popular Spanish game show 'Per-Lunko'
25. Return armadillo
26. Weep for the disenchanted
27. Practise noted 'startled' Dali expression
28. Patent noted 'startled' Dali expression
29. Intimidate a guinea fowl

1. Wake
2. Discard Dali's sleeping shroud
3. Wash face in the blood of a crab
4. Eat a single wren's egg
5. Short clavis
6. Dali's moustache regimen
7. Dress outrageously
8. Call stockbroker
9. Leave dwelling
10. Buy lobster, get discount, you are Dali
11. Buy leash as above
12. Startle ordinaries with lobster on leash
13. Dispose of lobster, return leash for store credit
14. Dance frantically
15. Rest
16. Commence triptych featuring lake of oil and weird face
17. Copyright initial triptych sketches
18. Claim to be magnetic
19. Lunch on entire roasted prawn
20. Change outfit (more outrageous)
21. Approve Dali tea-towel range
22. Appear on popular Spanish game show 'Ter-Lunko'
23. Distress fellow guests with armadillo
24. Invoice for appearance on popular Spanish gameshow 'Ter-Lunko'
25. Return armadillo
26. Weep for the disenchanted
27. Practise noted startled Dali expression
28. Patent noted startled Dali expression
29. Intimidate a guinea fowl
30. Run to the sea and scream
31. Collect ludicrous hat in the shape of a pig
32. Insist on discount for hat in the shape of a pig
33. Parade with hat
34. Film Wet Wipes commercial
35. Feed ocelot
36. Emerge from a man-sized egg
37. Collect bits for sculpture (wheelbarrow, mannequin head, etc.)
38. Nap
39. Finish triptych
40. Send triptych to Dali Museum
41. Invoice Dali Museum for Triptych
42. Deposit cheques
43. Dinner with the Finnish Ambassador and Neil Sedaka
44. Invoice above for meal
45. Appear on popular Spanish chat show 'Charlar!'
46. Only speak in a series of squeaks and sit on a large leather-egg
47. Invoice for appearance on popular Spanish chat show 'Charlar!'
48. Cocktails at La Plancha
49. Insist on having cocktail named after Dali
50. Insist on not paying for cocktail named after Dali
51. Perform genuflexion to the moon
52. Copyright genuflexion
53. Buy paint for tomorrow
54. Return to dwelling
55. Pretend to have scarabs for legs
56. Disassemble moustache
57. Sheathe Dali in Dali's sleeping shroud
58. Pray
59. Sleep
60. Dream
61. Invoice

30. Run to the sea and scream
31. Collect ludicrous hat in the shape of a fig
32. Insist on discount for hat in the shape of a fig
33. Parade with hat
34. Film Wet Wipes commercial
35. Feed ocelot
36. Emerge from a man-sized egg
37. Collect bits for sculpture (wheelbarrow, mannequin head, etc.)
38. Nap
39. Finish triptych
40. Send triptych to Dali Museum
41. Invoice Dali Museum for triptych
42. Deposit cheques
43. Dinner with the Finnish Ambassador and Neil Sedaka
44. Invoice above for meal
45. Appear on popular Spanish chat show 'Charlar!'
46. Only speak in a series of squeaks and sit on a large leather elk
47. Invoice for appearance on popular Spanish chat show 'Charlar!'
48. Cocktails at La Plancha
49. Insist on having cocktail named after Dali
50. Insist on not paying for cocktail named after Dali
51. Perform genuflexion to the moon
52. Copyright genuflexion
53. Buy paint for tomorrow
54. Return to dwelling
55. Pretend to have scarabs for legs
56. Disassemble moustache
57. Sheathe Dali in Dali's sleeping shroud
58. Pray
59. Sleep
60. Dream
61. Invoice

17th April 1908

Dear Baden-Powell,

Thank you so much for sending me a copy of your book *Scouting for Boys* and the accompanying letter informing me about the rapidly expanding Scout movement and appealing for donations to formalise this 'Boy Scouts' club.

This seems to be a highly worthy cause and one I would be delighted to be associated with. The sense of community, responsibility and discipline it attempts to encourage in our young people is surely to be commended.

I do have a very small number of concerns regarding the prospective venture. Before I put my name to it as a wholehearted supporter (as I am sure to become), and offer financial assistance, I was wondering if these could be addressed and possibly amended.

Namely, as it stands at the moment, I was wondering if there's a way to make it any less creepy, for the current proposal really creeps me out.

Perhaps I should explain myself. While obviously your intentions are entirely honourable and have nothing but the best welfare of the children in mind, I fear it may appear odd to certain parties. For instance, is it necessary for all the young boys to be constantly wearing shorts? It appears there is no provision for long trousers at all, even in the winter months or at formal events. Of course, shorts are the most practical of garments allowing for ventilation, comfort and ease of access. Which is where the problems may arise. Perhaps the wearing of these items could be encouraged without making it entirely mandatory, just to reduce the creepiness slightly?

I was also fairly creeped out by the notion of the 'camps' you suggest. From what I gather, the children will be taken into the wilderness, disabling any contact with relatives or guardians and instead be under the supervision of a man or 'Scout Master', who will be unknown to them. While of course I commend the encouragement of woodcrafts and survival techniques, I fear some misunderstanding may occur with a grown man leading a number of small boys in shorts to an undisclosed location for the purpose of, as you put it, 'fun, rigorous physical activity and self-exploration' and a certain creepy sub-text will be applied.

There is also a distinctly creepy element with the focus on 'cleanliness'. It is referred to frequently in your guidebook, almost to a degree any normal, well-adjusted human would consider disturbing. Throughout the work I noticed references to tidiness, comfort, 'how to grow strong', 'how to stay clean', 'microbes and how to find them', 'aquatics', 'practices in self-improvement' and washing tips. While I recognise the fundamental importance of body maintenance, I feel the children that the movement is aimed at will probably have been taught some basic degree of personal hygiene and all this banging on about being washed is ... well ... a bit creepy.

In the wrong hands, your guidebook may be perceived as some sort of manual to create an army of be-shorted, uniformed children, obsessed with cleanliness and gambolling in the woods with strange men, who may or may not be bearded. Obviously all the stuff about strangling small animals and disposing of dead bodies is perfectly acceptable. It's just all those other elements that I found really, really creepy. If you could remedy this, a cheque will be with you in due course.

Yours in potential interest,
Sir Charles Hadding

P.S. I am hoping that the 'woggles' that you mention are not the same as the ones that were inflicted upon me in boarding school. If so, this should also be looked at. Very creepy.

ART GARFUNKEL
WRITES TO
VAMPIRE WEEKEND

8th May 2009

Hi Guys!

This is Arthur Garfunkel. You might know me better as Art Garfunkel. But you can just call me Artie.

I was being driven to see my business manager the other day here in beautiful Los Angeles and the radio was on (I usually hate hearing music other than my own as it just messes with my head, you know?) and I was just about to tell whoever to switch it off when I caught something that just blew me away.

'Wow,' I said to my assistant, 'this is a hot new sound.'

At first I thought it must be something by my former singing partner who shall not be named (Paul Simon) but I had my people look into it and they told me about your rock band The Vampire Weekend!

I gotta say, old Artie Garfunkel loves what you are doing. It's so beautiful to hear such hip, young players who are not afraid to wear their musical influences out there on their sleeves. I got my other assistant to dash out and get your album, then had her download it onto my Pod and I checked it out when I was doing my Hot Rock Pilates. Wow! I absolutely loved most of it.

Now, I know you love that other guy's (Paul Simon) stuff. That is really obvious from your sweet new sound. The Graceland vibe is all over your LP. But, and this is an old musical head talking at ya, the journey that led you to my old musical amigo and all that African stuff took a hell of a detour via old Artie G. Don't get me wrong, he's done some great work on his own and you guys have obviously picked up on that vibe he's been hanging with for the last few years, with mixed results ('The Capeman').

Now listen, I don't want this letter to be all about 'you know who' (Paul Simon). He is an incredibly talented guy. I should know, he worked with me for many, many years. No one can play the old six-string acoustic guitar like that little dude. But you know, the second anyone talks to me about anything, the name Paul Simon instantly appears. You know when we last made a record together? 1970! Since then I've had a whole substantial life and career of my own. Movies, specials, tours of Buddhist centers and many, many

Art Garfunkel

8th May 2009

Hi Guys!

This is Arthur Garfunkel. You might know me better as Art Garfunkel. But you can just call me Artie.

I was being driven to see my business manager the other day here in beautiful Los Angeles and the radio was on (I usually hate hearing music other than my own as it just messes with my head, you know?) and I was just about to tell whoever to switch it off when I caught something that just blew me away.

'Wow,' I said to my assistant, 'this is a hot new sound.'

At first I thought it must be something by my former singing partner who shall not be named (Paul Simon) but I had my people look into it and they told me about your rock band The Vampire Weekend!

I gotta say, old Artie Garfunkel loves what you are doing. It's so beautiful to hear such hip, young players who are not afraid to wear their musical influences out there on their sleeves. I got my other assistant to dash out and get your album, then had her download it onto my Pod and I checked it out when I was doing my Hot Rock Pilates. Wow! I absolutely loved most of it.

Now, I know you love that other guy's (Paul Simon) stuff. That is really obvious from your sweet new sound. The Graceland vibe is all over your LP. But, and this is an old musical head talking at ya, the journey that led you to my old musical amigo and all that African stuff took a hell of a detour via old Artie G. Don't get me wrong, he's done some great work on his own and you guys have obviously picked up on that vibe he's been hanging with for the last few years, with mixed results (The Capeman).

Now listen, I don't want this letter to be all about 'you know who' (Paul Simon). He is an incredibly talented guy. I should know, he worked with me for many, many years. No one can play the old six string acoustic guitar like that little dude. But you know, the second anyone talks to me about anything, the name Paul Simon instantly appears. You know when we last made a record together? 1970! Since then I've had a whole substantial life and career of my own. Movies, specials, tours of Buddhist centers and many, many Simon and Garfunkel reunion shows. But, check this out. If you thought Paul Simon had some chops, wait until you hear what Artie Garfunkel has to offer.

I know what you're thinking. Bright Eyes, right? I mean, sure, it is a classic tune. And it put a couple of my kids through college. But if musical magpies (feel free to use that) like yourselves want to take on a few more divergent, groovy influences that don't exploit a bunch of Africans, there is some great Art Garfunkel stuff out there. (Excuse me if you're already aware of all my oeuvre. Humility is a noted sin of mine).

Take a trip through some of my solo stuff and I think you'll be pleasantly surprised. I even won a Grammy for Best Children's Album. How many children's Grammys has Paul Simon got? About one less than Artie Garfunkel, that's how many.

Look, if you want proof, just Google me and you'll see I've produced most of my solo albums and from 2007 onwards I have been writing my own songs as well. And if you want that Artie Garfunkel sheen on your next release, now you've exhausted the sub-Paul Simon sound, just hit me up. I've got a great little studio set up here and the room sounds amazing. Huey Lewis and JD Souther have remarked at the quality of the acoustics and both have considered recording demos here.

I'm a busy dude, so you'll need to give me plenty of lead-time, but I would love to give a leg-up to some young rockers like yourselves. Production, co-writing, some general sort of vibe stuff, anything you need. Or if you just want to hang and rap with me about this crazy business called show, then hey, that's cool too.

OK cool, gotta split, but listen, just contact my assistant (number included) when you feel like jamming. Honestly, it seems like the perfect fit to me. Ditch all that 'You Can Call Me Al' (a song about me, I assume) stuff and jump on the Artie Garfunkel bandwagon. You never know, you might just make it.

Your pal,

Artie

P.S. You'll need to change your name. You'll never get anywhere with a name like that.

Simon and Garfunkel reunion shows. But, check this out. If you thought Paul Simon had some chops, wait until you hear what Artie Garfunkel has to offer.

I know what you're thinking. 'Bright Eyes', right? I mean, sure, it is a classic tune. And it put a couple of my kids through college. But if musical magpies (feel free to use that) like yourselves want to take on a few more divergent, groovy influences that don't exploit a bunch of Africans, there is some great Art Garfunkel stuff out there. (Excuse me if you're already aware of all my oeuvre. Humility is a noted sin of mine.)

Take a trip through some of my solo stuff and I think you'll be pleasantly surprised. I even won a Grammy for Best Children's Album. How many children's Grammys has Paul Simon got? About one less than Artie Garfunkel, that's how many.

Look, if you want proof, just Google me and you'll see I've produced most of my solo albums and from 2007 onwards I have been writing my own songs as well. And if you want that Artie Garfunkel sheen on your next release, now you've exhausted the sub-Paul Simon sound, just hit me up. I've got a great little studio set up here and the room sounds amazing. Huey Lewis and JD Souther have remarked at the quality of the acoustics and both have considered recording demos here.

I'm a busy dude, so you'll need to give me plenty of lead-time, but I would love to give a leg-up to some young rockers like yourselves. Production, co-writing, some general sort of vibe stuff, anything you need. Or if you just want to hang and rap with me about this crazy business called show, then hey, that's cool too.

OK cool, gotta split, but listen, just contact my assistant (number included) when you feel like jamming. Honestly, it seems like the perfect fit to me. Ditch all that 'You Can Call Me Al' (a song about me, I assume) stuff and jump on the Artie Garfunkel bandwagon. You never know, you might just make it.

Your pal,
Artie

P.S. You'll need to change your name. You'll never get anywhere with a name like that.

24th May 14?1

Ok, boss, here's why I think you shouldn't burn me.

1. PR. No matter what beef you've got with me, and what went down in the heat of the... gaze. Sure, you can say I was a traitor and a witch and anything else you can... Public relations fiasco in my view. If you think you can handle the fallout, then the...

2. Payback. I know you didn't really buy all that 'on a mission from God who speaks...' but crazier things have happened. Do you really want to take that risk? Yeah, you...

3. Damage to the environment. I'm not just talking about all the polluting smoke... assuming this won't be a discreet affair, so you'll be building a pretty major structure... erosion, stuff like that. Again, more things to piss off God, as well as the local power... of stable. Even if you do put aside the environmental concerns, you'll have to go thro... have security concerns, policing, seating, toilets. All of those cramped villages will want... Plus, do you know how hard it is to burn a person? We're mainly made... if you're up there trying to get me started with a big crowd, who are clearly annoyed (a...

5. Information... Look, I am willing to spill anything you want. Maybe I... Or some dirt on the King himself? He seems very fond of a particular stable boy?...

6. Potential. You may have noticed that I'm known as the Maid of Orleans not the... blunt end of a burning. Not exactly a well-rounded life. I've got a lot of love to gi... become a top-notch pastry chef or some kind of great composer creating music that... we didn't burn that girl or boy, my life is lacking in entertainment, maybe if we...

In conclusion: If you have no interest in your image, your relationship... But, if you want to do the right thing, just leave that cell door ope...

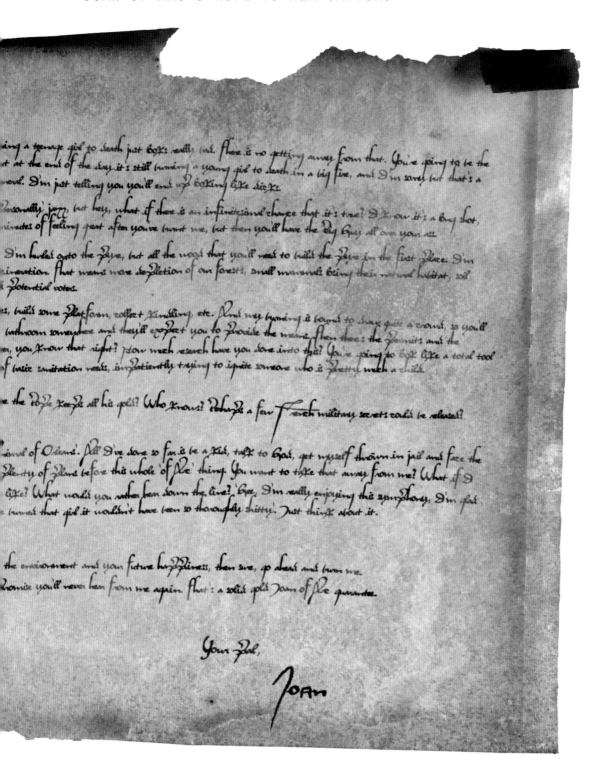

...ing a teenage girl to death just looks really bad. There is no getting away from that. You're going to be the ...t at the end of the day it's still burning a young girl to death in a big fire, and I'm sorry but that's a ...real. I'm just telling you you'll end up looking like dicks.

...Personally jarry, but hey, what if there is an infinitesimal chance that it's true? I know it's a long shot, ...inutes of feeling great after you've burnt me, but then you'll have the big boss all over your ass.

...I'm hurled onto the pyre, but all the wood that you'll need to build the pyre in the first place. I'm ...einvestion that means more depletion of our forests, small mammals losing their natural habitat, soil ...& potential voters.

...es, build some platform, collect kindling etc. And my burning is bound to draw quite a crowd, so you'll ...bathroom somewhere and they'll expect you to provide the mains. Then there's the permits and the ...en, you know that right? How much research have you done into this? You're going to look like a total tool ...of basic sanitation needs, impatiently trying to ignite someone who is pretty much a child.

...e the Pope keeps all his gold? Who knows? Perhaps a few French military secrets could be released?

...ianal of Orleans. All I've done so far is be a kid, talk to God, get myself thrown in jail and face the ...plenty of plans before this whole 'of Arc' thing. You want to take that away from me? What if I ...alike? What would you rather been doing, like? Hey, I'm really enjoying this symphony, I'm glad ...e burnt that girl it wouldn't have been so thoroughly shitty. Just think about it.

...the environment and your future happiness, then sure, go ahead and burn me. ...Promise you'll never hear from me again. That's a solid gold Joan of Arc guarantee.

Your Pal,

Joan

29th May 1431

OK, look, here's why I think you shouldn't burn me.

1. PR. No matter what beef you've got with me, and what went down in the heat of battle, burning a teenage girl to death just looks really bad. There is no getting away from that. You're going to be the bad guys. Sure, you can say I was a traitor and a witch and anything else you can drum up, but at the end of the day it's still burning a young girl to death in a big fire, and I'm sorry but that's a public relations fiasco in my view. If you think you can handle the fallout, then that's your funeral. I'm just telling you you'll end up looking like dicks.

2. Payback. I know you didn't really buy all that 'on a mission from God who speaks to me personally' jazz, but hey, what if there is an infinitesimal chance that it's true? I know it's a long shot, but crazier things have happened. Do you really want to take that risk? Yeah, you'll have ten minutes of feeling great after you've burnt me, but then you'll have the Big Guy all over your ass.

3. Damage to the environment. I'm not just talking about all the polluting smoke created once I'm hurled onto the pyre, but all the wood that you'll need to build the pyre in the first place. I'm assuming this won't be a discreet affair, so you'll be building a pretty major structure for my incineration. That means more depletion of our forests, small mammals losing their natural habitat, soil erosion, stuff like that. Again, more things to piss off God, as well as the local government and potential voters.

4. Hassle. Even if you do put aside the environmental concerns, you'll have to go chop down trees, build some platform, collect kindling, etc. And my burning is bound to draw quite a crowd, so you'll have security concerns, policing, seating, touts. All of those enraged villagers will need to go to the bathroom somewhere and they'll expect you to provide the means. Then there's the permits and the paperwork.

Plus, do you know how hard it is to burn a person? We're mainly made up of water, you know that right? How much research have you done into this? You're going to look like a total tool if you're up there trying to get me started with a big crowd, who are already angered by the lack of basic sanitation needs, impatiently trying to ignite someone who is pretty much a child.

5. Information. Look, I am willing to spill anything you want. Maybe I know where the Pope keeps all his gold? Who knows? Perhaps a few French military secrets could be released? Or some dirt on the King himself? He seems very fond of a particular stable boy? Just saying.

6. Potential. You may have noticed that I'm known as the 'Maid of Orleans' not the 'Party Animal of Orleans'. All I've done so far is be a kid, talk to God, get myself thrown in jail and face the blunt end of a burning. Not exactly a well-rounded life. I've got a lot of love to give. I had plenty of plans before this whole 'of Arc' thing. You want to take that away from me? What if I become a top-notch pastry chef or some kind of great composer creating music that you really like? What would you rather hear down the line? 'Gee, I'm really enjoying this symphony, I'm glad we didn't burn that girl' or 'Boy, my life is lacking in entertainment, maybe if we hadn't have burned that girl it wouldn't have been so thoroughly shitty'. Just think about it.

In conclusion: If you have no interest in your image, your relationship with God, the environment and your future happiness, then sure, go ahead and burn me. But, if you want to do the right thing, just leave that cell door open and I promise you'll never hear from me again. That's a solid gold Joan of Arc guarantee.

Your pal,
Joan

---

1. Remember, you'll soon be a millionaire, so ACT like a millionaire. Point out salient things with your cane. Hook your thumbs into your waistcoat and lean back in a jovial way. (NB: buy one of those waistcoats with dollar signs on it – the EXPENSIVE kind.) Leave the nerd glasses at home. Try that monocle instead.

2. Begin all your sentences with 'Did I mention ...' as in 'Did I mention all the money I happen to make with the computer stuff?' You'll sound authentic and classy. As does using the word 'happen'. If they question you, don't be too specific. Remember chicks tend to glaze over when you explain the intricacies of operating systems. Keep it light.

3. If Headlock gets you in his customary headlock, don't flail your spindly arms and legs in a panicky manner while yelping and gasping. You're a RICH and POWERFUL business mogul – act with dignity and attempt to fend off his aggression with witty ripostes. Memorize a few jokes and try to learn that limerick. Don't bite him, that just makes things worse. As a last resort offer him stock (NB: take some stock). If that doesn't work, mention the Microsoft Killer Cyborg Program (MKCP).

4. Don't try to dance. But if you are forced to dance, try to dance with ELEGANCE. Remember to search for 'elegant dancing tips' at the library.

5. Avoid everyone you were in the chess/math/D&D club with. Especially Kyle. If they approach you, shield yourself with your millionaire's cape (NB: buy cape). They'll just want to talk to you about computer stuff. Even though you'll really want to do this, resist.

6. Be sure to buy the BIGGEST cigars you can find (if the drugstore ones aren't large enough, see what the joke shop has). Practice smoking them before the event – perhaps get smaller cigars to practice on. If you gag and choke, claim it's something they do in Continental Europe, which you observed when you were there at an important computer conference.

be a millionaire, so ACT like a millionaire. Point out
cane. Hook your thumbs into your waistcoat and lean back
one of those waistcoats with dollar signs on it - the
e nerd glasses at home. Try that monocle instead.

es with "Did I mention …" as in "Did I mention all the
ith the computer stuff?" You'll sound authentic and classy.
happen". If they question you, don't be too specific.
glaze over when you explain the intricacies of operating

n his customary headlock, don't flail your spindly arms and
while yelping and gasping. You're a RICH and POWERFUL
dignity and attempt to fend off his aggression with witty
jokes and try to learn that limerick. Don't bite him, that
As a last resort offer him stock. (NB: take some stock). If
the Microsoft Killer Cyborg Program (MKCP).

t if you are forced to dance, try to dance with ELEGAN
elegant   library.

re in   lub with. Especially Kyle.
yours   aire's cape (NB: buy cape).
to you   f. Even though you'll really

7. Practice smiling. Attempt to show either your upper or BOTH AT ONCE. Brush teeth twice. Buy gum.

8. Try not to go to the toilet (see Headlock, above). If yo stock in there with you.

9. If all else fails, fake an important phone call on your phone, provided by your big computer business. (NB: get bu reading Bill Gates, Chief Idea-gineer.)

10. When you see Debbie – DON'T PANIC. Don't cry. Don't vom vomit. Remember your recent presentation to the Microsoft I expressions on the investors' faces when you got over-nerv that one is going to occur then try to vomit rather than c it on the richness of your mogul's diet. As you approach De NONCHALANT. Beware of drool and spittle. Don't propose imme (Not with operating systems talk, see above.) If she starts ɪst time), laugh along (remember thumbs/waistcoat), then fa Run like you are running towards a limo.

o not return, get on stage, push ⅃' ʼ ʼ ɴ ɹnfairness of life. Don't point ou ʼ ɪ ǂ though you have a cane, which ⅃Ꮴorgs, don't offer stock and don't d ɪ is very moving (according to Mom).

12. Remember, hand out the business c.

7. Practice smiling. Attempt to show either your upper or lower set of teeth. Not BOTH AT ONCE. Brush teeth twice. Buy gum.

8. Try not to go to the toilet (see Headlock, above). If you have to, take some stock in there with you.

9. If all else fails, fake an important phone call on your businessman's travel phone, provided by your big computer business. (NB: get business card printed up reading Bill Gates, Chief Idea-gineer.)

10. When you see Debbie – DON'T PANIC. Don't cry. Don't vomit. And don't cry and vomit. Remember your recent presentation to the Microsoft board and the harrowed expressions on the investors' faces when you got over-nervous. If it's inevitable that one is going to occur then try to vomit rather than cry. Then you can blame it on the richness of your mogul's diet. As you approach Debbie, try to be NONCHALANT. Beware of drool and spittle. Don't propose immediately. Lead up to it. (Not with operating systems talk, see above.) If she starts to laugh at you (like last time), laugh along (remember thumbs/ waistcoat), then fake a heart attack and run. Run like you are running towards a limo.

11. Do not return, get on stage, push the singer aside and make that speech about the unfairness of life. Don't point out people in the crowd who have held you back (even though you have a cane, which would make this easier). Don't mention the cyborgs, don't offer stock and don't do your MIME about LONELINESS, even though it is very moving (according to Mom).

12. Remember, hand out the business cards. And don't forget to have fun!

EDGAR ALLAN POE VS. THE BALTIMORE SANITATION DEPT

4th September 1848

Sir,

This is now the fourth occasion that I have found myself writing in regards to the provision of refuse disposal at my domicile on Amity Street.

As you should be well aware, this detritus should be collected during Thursday mornings, on a weekly basis. However, this seemingly perfunctory event never appears to occur. And when a miracle is granted and these purveyors of trash do attend, there is often as much of the material strewn about my property as contained in the conveyance offered for this purpose. It's almost as if these rubbish-mongers are purposefully befouling my perimeter.

Now sir, I have tried cajoling you, pleading with you, flattering you and even, God help me, reasoning with you in an ill-fated attempt to improve your performance. I'm afraid my patience has worn rather thin and I feel that my only course of action is to delve into the unsavory.

I hate to threaten, Mr Pargeter, but as you know I am a writer of some merit and was recently dubbed the 'Master of the Macabre' by a leading periodical. This estimation is not disingenuous, my dear sir. I am extremely macabre. Possibly too macabre, sometimes. I don't believe you would wish to discover the lengths and depths of my macabre imagination and unleash its contents upon you. But I fear your continued ignorance compels me to do so.

Let me provide a hypothetical. Perhaps a letter were to reach you, unsigned, scripted in ink of the most fiendish crimson. Inside you would find a tale so chilling, so disturbing, so freaking macabre, your nightly sojourns would be forever affected. I feel an example may be necessary to fully make my meaning clear.

Wait! What was that noise? A strange creak behind you? But what of its source? Surely you're all alone in your lodgings? And no guest is expected, and the servants have the night off.

4th September 1848

Sirs

This is now the fourth occasion that I have found
myself writing in regards to the provision of refuse
disposed at my domicile on Leafy Street

As you should be well aware, this detritus should
be collected during Thursday mornings on a weekly basis
However, this seemingly perfunctory event never appears
to occur. And when a miracle is granted and there purveyors
of trash do attend, there is often as much of the mel arend
strewn about my property as contained in the conveyance
offered for this purpose. It is almost as of these rubbish
mongers are purposefully befouling my perimeter.

Now sirs I have tried cajoling you, pleading with your
flattering you and even God help me, reasoning with you in
an ill-fated attempt to improve your performance. I am
afraid my patience has worn rather thin and I feel that
my only course of action is to delve into the unsavory.

I hate to threaten Mr Pargeter, but as you know
I am a writer of some merit and was recently dubbed
the Master of the Macabre by a leading periodical. This
estimation is not disingenuous my dear sirs I am extremely
macabre. Possibly too macabre, sometimes I don't believe you
would wish to discover the lengths and depths of my macabre
imagination and unleash its contents upon you But I fear your
continued ignorance compels me to do so.

Let me provide a hypothetical. Perhaps a letter were to reach you, unsigned, scripted in ink of the most fiendish crimson. Inside you would find a tale so chilling, so disturbing, so freaking macabre your nightly sojourns would be forever affected. I feel an example may be necessary to fully make my meaning clear.

Wait! What was that noise? A strange creak behind you? But what of its source? Surely you're all alone in your lodgings? And no guest is expected, and the servants have the night off

Yes, not very nice is it? But look, it only gets worse, listen! Is that a scritch-scratching at my chambers window pane? Surely you are too paralysed with terror to countenance and yet you may go simply insane if you do not investigate. What could it be? A specter? A branch? Surely reading a letter describing such an incident would cloud your night-mares forever.

But our macabre adventure has just begun I can be way way more macabre. So macabre that a fixed grimace of agonizing misery would forever grace your visage

BATS! Oh yes, weren't expecting that were you? Nasty little things flapping and praying disturbing your hair and clothing with those leathery unnatural wings. How delectably macabre. Especially where I plan to place them, Mr Pargeter. Directly in the centre of your mind ghoulish, no?

Yes, not very nice is it? But look, it only gets worse. Listen! Is that a scritch-scratching at my chamber's windowpane? Surely you are too paralyzed with terror to countenance and yet you may go simply insane if you do not investigate. What could it be? A specter? A branch? Surely reading a letter describing such an incident would cloud your nightmares forever.

But our macabre adventure has just begun. I can be way, way more macabre. So macabre, that a fixed grimace of agonizing misery would forever grace your visage.

BATS! Oh yes, weren't expecting that were you? Nasty little things. Flapping and prying. Disturbing your hair and clothing with their leathery, unnatural wings. How delectably macabre. Especially where I plan to place them, Mr Pargeter. Directly in the centre of your mind. Ghoulish, no?

MORE BATS! THEY'RE IN YOUR HAIR! SQUEAKING! Just picture it, or a tale similar to this, expanded obviously, with even more bats, and perhaps a few moths, to inconvenience you. Your existence would be altered forever. Your hands shaking every time the letterbox was engaged. Is it more tales of horror? What have you done to deserve this?

Of course, all this macabre unpleasantness need never occur. Merely ensure that your sanitation aspect is rendered satisfactorily. All this proposed horror can be stowed safely within me and never be unleashed against you.

But if the situation were to persist: CREAKS! NOISES! BATS!

Think on,
Edgar Allan Poe

P.S. It may be more appropriate if you were to read the more macabre passages from above in a deep, 'spooky' voice, if you could be so kind.

MORE BATS! THEY'RE IN YOUR HAIR!
SQUEAKING! Just picture it, or a tale similar to this,
expanded obviously with even more bats, and perhaps a few
moths, to inconvenience you. Your existence would be altered
forever. Your hands shaking every time the letterbox was
engaged. Is it more tales of horror? What have you done to
deserve this?

Of course, all this macabre unpleasantness need never
occur if I were to ensure that your sanitation aspect is rendered
satisfactorily. All this proposed horror can be stowed
safely within me and never be unleashed against you.

But if the situation were to persist; CREAKS! NOISES!
BATS!

            Think on

            Edgar Allan Poe

P.S. It may be more appropriate if you were to read the
more macabre passages from above in a deep 'spooky' voice, if
you could be so kind.

23rd December 1888

Dear Vincent,

I have just received the gift you left for me, which appears to be various small portions of your ear.

Before I go any further can I just tell you: I LOVE IT! THANK YOU! THANK YOU! THANK YOU!!!

It is incredibly kind and thoughtful of you. I can't think of a more exciting present for a suitor to send to their prospective beau. I totally understand where you are coming from with all this. It's really great.

A girl in my profession tends to get sent a great deal of gifts and it can be tiring to receive endless amounts of the usual chocolates and flowers. Flowers soon perish and chocolates can make a girl fat! But a section of ear has no detrimental deficits whatsoever and can last a lifetime (if placed in some kind of preservative). It's really the ideal way for a gentleman to express his true feelings for a woman in a singular and unique fashion. Well done.

I've already shown the ear portion to a number of my girlfriends and all of them are green with envy. They too would love the attentions of a man willing to hack off part of himself as a testament to romance. Some have offered quite large sums to get the ear from me! But of course I would never part with it.

I'm thinking of mounting the flesh decoratively in some way. Perhaps as a necklace or brooch (earrings would probably be redundant). As well as writing to thank you, I was also wondering if you were planning to remove any other body parts in the near future? You see, I'd love to turn them into a matching set of some kind. The ear section alone is going to be fantastic, but coupled with another human portion, could well be spectacular. I don't know what you can spare? Perhaps a toe or a section of scalp? I'll leave it up to you. You're the artist.

145

23rd December 1888

...he gift you left for me, which appears to be various ...can. Before I go any further can I just tell you ...I. I❤️LOVE YOU. I❤️LOVE YOU!!!

...l and thoughtful of you. I can't think of a more exciting ...nitor to send to their prospective beau. I totally under... ...e coming from with all this. It's really great ...fession tends to get sent a great deal of gifts and it can be ...ndless amounts of the usual chocolates and flowers. Your ...nd chocolates can make a girl fat. But a section of ear has ...d deficits whatsoever and can last a lifetime (if placed in ...reservative). It's really the ideal way for a gentleman to ex... ...lings for a woman in a singular and unique fashion. Well done. ...um the ear portion to a number of my girlfriends and all of ...on with envy. They too would love the attentions of a man ...ce off part of himself as a testament to romance. Some have ...e large ones to get the ear from me. But of course, I would ...with it.

...ing of mounting the flesh decoratively in some way. Perhaps as a ...a brooch (earrings would probably be redundant). It's well as ...to thank you, I was also wondering if you were planning to ...y other body parts in the near future. You see, I'd love to turn ...o a matching set of some kind. The ear section alone is going to ...ties, but coupled with another human portion, could well be spec... ...I don't know what you can spare? Perhaps a toe or a section of scalp? ...e it up to you. You're the artist. ...ly completely understand if that sounds unreasonable. Are you'd ...wait until the stitches are removed before you take anything else off ...let me know either way and I'll tell the jeweller what to do. ...ing to decide what I can send you in return. Due to my work com... ...ents, part of myself are probably out of the question. But I thought ...f something crafty? Like a collage or a quilt? Let's have a chat about ...hen you get out of the hospital. I'll try and pop by and visit you if I ...d the brothel early. ...ere forming outside my room. But thank you ...can't wait to see you and whisper

Obviously I completely understand if that sounds unreasonable. Or you'd like to wait until the stitches are removed before you take anything else off. But let me know either way and I'll tell the jeweller what to do.

I'm trying to decide what I can send you in return! Due to my work commitments, parts of myself are probably out of the question. But I thought perhaps something crafty? Like a collage or a quilt? Let's have a chat about it when you get out of the hospital. I'll try to pop by and visit you if I can get out of the brothel early.

OK, got to dash, there's a queue forming outside my room. But thank you again for your lovely gift and I can't wait to see you and whisper sweet nothings into what is left of your ear.

Love,
Rachel

23rd July 1977

Dear Daniel,

Thank you so much for writing to the Blue Peter team. I am the lady in charge of everyone. Quite a chore sometimes! And thank you for sending us your notes and diagrammatic explanation for your very special rocket! It amused us all greatly. I'm so sorry to hear that your mother feels the planned experiment is far too dangerous to undertake and that attaching a rubber hose to the gas cooker and using it as your rocket's primary fuel source would be problematic. And I am sure others around you have offered similar warnings concerning your scientific project.

To which I say poppycock! Chase your dreams, Daniel. The only way to find out if your gerbil can reach orbit is to pressurise that gas, relay it into an air-tight metal tube and then ignite it with a large flame or burning tube of newspaper (standing at a safe distance of course, though not so far that you can't observe and take notes).

None of our boldest endeavours, exciting discoveries or life-changing inventions would ever have been made if the gentlemen concerned heeded the advice of parents, peers and the express instructions of the National Gas Board. The solution is simple. Ensure that all those fuddy-duddies determined to thwart your efforts are absent when you embark on your exceptional adventure. Wait until they are asleep or have popped out for the day, and then proceed.

So, I insist you persist with gusto young Daniel, that is the Blue Peter way. There's a badge in it for you if you get little Snuffles higher than 40ft. Please do let us know of your findings. Who knows, if they are particularly spectacular perhaps we can feature you on the show, if not for your invention, then as a beneficiary of one of our charity campaigns.

Yours,
Biddy

BRITISH TELEVISION CENTRE
WOOLAND ROAD LONDON W13 77J
TELEPHONE 01-744 800 TELEGRAMS: TELEVISION TELEX

Ref: CC   23rd July 1977

Dear Daniel,

    Thank you so much for writing to the Blue Peter team. I am the
lady in charge of everyone. Quite a chore sometimes!
And thank you for sending us your notes and diagrammatic explanation
for your very special rocket! It amused us all greatly. I'm so sorry
to hear that your mother feels the planned experiment is far too
dangerous to undertake and that attaching a rubber hose to the gas
cooker and using it as your rocket's primary fuel source would be
problematic. And I am sure others around you have offered similar
warnings concerning your scientific project.

To which I say poppycock! Chase your dreams, Daniel. The only way to
find out if your gerbil can reach orbit is to pressurise that gas,
relay it into an air-tight metal tube and then ignite it with a
large flame or burning tube of newspaper (standing at a safe
distance of course, though not so far that you can't observe and
take notes).

None of our boldest endeavours, exciting discoveries or life-changing inventions would ever have been made if the gentlemen concerned
heeded the advice of parents, peers and the express instructions of
the National Gas Board. The solution is simple. Ensure that all
those fuddy-duddies determined to thwart your efforts are absent
when you embark on your exceptional adventure. Wait until they are
asleep or have popped out for the day, and then proceed.

So, I insist you persist with gusto young Daniel, that is the Blue
Peter way. There's a badge in it for you if you get little Snuffles
higher than 40ft. Please do let us know of your findings. Who knows,
if they are particularly spectacular perhaps we can feature you on
the show, if not for your invention, then as a beneficiary of one of
our charity campaigns.

Yours,

Biddy

149

PEGI,

IF YOU GO TO THE STORE, PLEASE COULD YOU GET ME THE FOLLOWING ITEMS:

1. ONIONS. RED ONIONS. RED LIKE THE PAINTWORK OF THAT 1959 LINCOLN CONTINENTAL THAT I OWNED AROUND 1981. THAT WAS A BEAUTIFUL AUTOMOBILE WE JUST USED TO SHIMMY DOWN THE FREEWAY, MY OLD DOG CLAUDE SITTING BESIDE ME. CLAUDE WAS A GREAT LITTLE HOUND, PART BEAGLE, PART CHOW, PART ESKIMO I THINK. WE'D HEAD OUT IN THE CONNIE AND PARK UP AT THE EDGE OF THE PRAIRIE, ME WATCHING THE WIND, CLAUDE LOOKING OUT FOR RABBITS. HE LOVED RABBITS. I LOVE RABBITS. I'D SIT THERE, NEXT TO CLAUDE, AND THINK, YOU KNOW, SONGS ARE KIND OF LIKE RABBITS. YOU GOT TO BE PATIENT, LET THEM COME TO YOU, DON'T FRIGHTEN THEM AWAY. I REMEMBER BEING NAKED WITH ELVIS AND NINA SIMONE, SMOKING OPIUM IN LAHORE AND SAYING SOMETHING SIMILAR ... ANYWAY BACK TO THE RABBITS. SONGS ARE LIKE RABBITS. IN FACT, SONGS ARE LIKE A LOT OF SMALL MAMMALS. HAMSTERS, FOXES, STOATS, CHIPMUNKS, SLOTHS, BATS, GERBILS, BADGERS, MARMOSETS, VOLES, MICE, SHETLAND PONIES, RATS, WHITE RATS, WATER RATS, BROWN RATS, BLACK RATS, SMALL RATS, BIG RATS, BEAVERS AND PRAIRIE DOGS. MY OLD DOG CLAUDE LOVED THE PRAIRIE, CLAUDE AND ME, WE'D BE OUT THERE, SOMETIMES IN THE CONNIE, SOMETIMES IN MY 1948 BUICK ROADMASTER THAT I GOT BACK IN 81, JUST OLD BLUE AND I. OLD BLUE WAS ANOTHER GREAT DOG I HAD. PART HUSKY, PART THE DOG THAT GRAHAM NASH USED TO OWN, ANYWAY, I USED TO HOP STRAIGHT INTO MY 1956 CROWN VICTORIA, THE ONE I BOUGHT IN 1981, AND WE'D HEAD OUT INTO THE CANYON AND JUST LISTEN TO THE SILENCE. AND I THOUGHT, IF ONLY IT WAS POSSIBLE TO ATTAIN THE SAME SOUND CLARITY WITH A COMMERCIAL DIGITAL MUSIC DEVICE. IT WAS THEN I STARTED WORKING ON THE SOUNDSOURCE 5000 OR THE SOSO, AS IT WILL BE KNOWN INTERNATIONALLY. IT IS GOING TO REVOLUTIONIZE THE MUSIC INDUSTRY. NEVER WILL MUSIC BE HEARD WITH SUCH PRECISION. ONCE, JOHN LENNON REVEALED TO ME THE SECRETS OF GREAT SONGWRITING ... ANYWAY YOU'LL BE ABLE TO HEAR HIS SONGS AND MANY OTHERS WITH PERFECTLY REPRODUCED CADENCE THANKS TO THE SOUNDSOURCE 5000 OR THE SOSO, AS IT WILL BE KNOWN GLOBALLY. BECAUSE SONGS DESERVE RESPECT, THEY ARE LIKE RABBITS. RABBITS DESERVE RESPECT.

YOU'VE GOT TO TICKLE THEM JUST RIGHT. TICKLE THEM, DON'T SCARE THEM, BECAUSE WHEN I SAY RABBITS, I MEAN SONGS. SONGS ARE LIKE RABBITS AND THEY ARE ALSO LIKE SHREWS, MEERKATS, SQUIRRELS, BUSH BABIES, OTTERS, GUINEAPIGS, HARES, FERRETS, MOLES, SMALL CATS, OCELOTS, AND MOST IMPORTANTLY, RABBITS. MY SONGS ARE LIKE

RABBITS AND THEY ARE ALSO LIKE MY DOGS IN SO MUCH AS MY DOGS ARE LIKE MY CHILDREN, WITH MY CHILDREN BEING LIKE MY CARS AND MY CARS, WELL, THEY REMIND ME OF MY TRUCKS. THE BEST TRUCK I EVER OWNED WAS A 1969 FORD F-100 RANGER, SOLD TO ME BY JIMI HENDRIX JUST BEFORE HE FAKED HIS OWN DEATH. ANYWAY, I LOVED THAT TRUCK. LOVED IT LIKE A CHILD OR A SONG OR A DOG. SKIPPY, A GREAT OLD DOG OF MINE, WOULD HOP IN THE BACK OF THE 1956 CHEVY 3100 THAT I GOT IN 1981 AND I'D THROW ON MY FAVORITE PLAID SHIRT. I LOVED THAT SHIRT. IT HAD PRESS-STUDS AND THE 'POP' THEY MADE WHEN YOU BUTTONED IT UP WAS JUST REMARKABLE. ANYWAY I THOUGHT, 'I WONDER IF THERE WOULD EVER BE ANY SOUND TECHNOLOGY THAT COULD REPRODUCE THE BEAUTIFUL NOISE THOSE PRESS-STUDS MAKE?' RIGHT THERE AND THEN I STARTED THINKING ABOUT THE SOUNDSOURCE 5000, OR THE SOSO AS IT WILL BE REGARDED THE WORLD OVER. IF ONLY THERE COULD BE A PORTABLE MUSIC DEVICE WHERE MY SONGS (WHICH ARE LIKE RABBITS) COULD BE HEARD IN MY CARS, WHILE WEARING A PLAID SHIRT AND ENJOYED BY MY DOGS (WHO LIKE RABBITS AND SONGS, AND SONGS WHICH ARE LIKE RABBITS) AND BE PERFECT. LIKE A TRAIN. I RECALL THE MOST IMPORTANT, LIFE CHANGING ADVICE I EVER GOT FROM THE GREAT BOB DYLAN HIMSELF. ANYWAY, I DIGRESS, I LIKE TRUCKS.

2. WALNUTS

THANKS

SHAKEY

Pegi,

If you go to the store, please could you get me the following items:

1. Onions. Red onions. Red like the paintwork of that 1959 Lincoln Continental that I owned around 1981. That was a beautiful automobile. We just used to shimmy down the freeway, my old dog Claude sitting beside me. Claude was a great little hound, part beagle, part chow, part Eskimo I think. We'd head out in the Connie and park up at the edge of the prairie, me watching the wind, Claude looking out for rabbits. He loved rabbits. I love rabbits. I'd sit there, next to Claude, and think, you know, songs are kind of like rabbits. You got to be patient, let them come to you, don't frighten them away. I remember being naked with Elvis and Nina Simone, smoking opium in Lahore and saying something similar ... anyway back to the rabbits. Songs are like rabbits. In fact, songs are like a lot of small mammals. Hamsters, foxes, stoats, chipmunks, sloths, bats, gerbils, badgers, marmosets, voles, mice, Shetland ponies, rats, white rats, water rats, brown rats, black rats, small rats, big rats, beavers and prairie dogs. My old dog Claude loved the prairie. Claude and me, we'd be out there, sometimes in the Connie, sometimes in my 1948 Buick Roadmaster that I got back in 81, just Old Blue and I. Old Blue was another great dog I had. Part husky, part the dog that Graham Nash used to own. Anyway, I used to hop straight into my 1956 Crown Victoria, the one I bought in 1981, and we'd head out into the canyon and just listen to the silence. And I thought, if only it was possible to attain the same sound clarity with a commercial digital music device. It was then I started working on the SoundSource 5000 or the Soso, as it will be known internationally. It is going to revolutionize the music industry. Never will music be heard with such precision. Once, John Lennon revealed to me the secrets of great songwriting ... anyway you'll be able to hear his songs and many others with perfectly reproduced cadence thanks to the SoundSource 5000 or the Soso, as it will be known globally. Because songs deserve respect, they are like rabbits. Rabbits deserve respect. You've got to tickle them just right. Tickle them, don't scare them, because when I say rabbits, I mean songs. Songs

are like rabbits. And they are also like shrews, meerkats, squirrels, bushbabies, otters, guinea pigs, hares, ferrets, moles, small cats, ocelots and most importantly, rabbits. My songs are like rabbits and they are also like my dogs in so much as my dogs are like my children, with my children being like my cars and my cars, well, they remind me of my trucks. The best truck I ever owned was a 1969 Ford F–100 Ranger, sold to me by Jimi Hendrix just before he faked his own death. Anyway, I loved that truck. Loved it like a child or a song or a dog. Skippy, a great old dog of mine, would hop in the back of the 1956 Chevy 3100 that I got in 1981 and I'd throw on my favorite plaid shirt. I loved that shirt. It had press-studs and the 'pop' they made when you buttoned it up was just remarkable. Anyway I thought, 'I wonder if there would ever be any sound technology that could reproduce the beautiful noise those press-studs make?' Right there and then I started thinking about the SoundSource 5000, or the Soso as it will be regarded the world over. If only there could be a portable music device where my songs (which are like rabbits) could be heard in my cars, while wearing a plaid shirt and enjoyed by my dogs (who like rabbits and songs, and songs which are like rabbits) and be perfect. Like a train. I recall the most important, life-changing advice I ever got from the great Bob Dylan himself. Anyway, I digress. I like trucks.

2. Walnuts

Thanks,
Shakey

Ask foreman again exactly why I'm not the foreman? (I'm a famous writer, etc.)

Then ask foreman if cake is provided.

Defence = Moustache. Prosecution = No moustache.

Defendant = Very shifty eyes, dirty finger nails, obvious wig. Awful.

Have been told the gentleman I thought was the defendant is actually the judge. Why is he up on a big chair in the middle of the room? Doesn't it make more sense for the criminal to be up there?

Correction. Defence = No moustache. Prosecution = Mole, foreign persuasion.

Why is everyone talking about the council? How are they involved?

Ask foreman if I can just say 'guilty' now so I can make it to the theatre on time.

Try to find out what happened when I nodded off, did I miss anything juicy I could use in a book?

Going to ignore all this 'forensic' palaver. Stuff and nonsense.
Gut instinct far more valuable.

Been told off for laughing sarcastically when the criminal speaks.
Can't I have an opinion?

Think judge is well aware of who I am. Jealous/possible sodomite.

JURY NOTES

Ask forman again exactly why I'm not the forman? (I'm a famous writer etc.)

Then ask forman if cake is provided

→ Defense = monstache

Prosecution = no monstache

---

defendant - very stubbly eyes, dirty fingernails, brown smug. AWFUL

Have been told by the gentleman I thought was the defendant is actually the judge. Why is he up on a huge box church the middle of the room? Doesn't it make more sense for the criminal to be up there?

Conviction —

Defence = No monstache
Prosecution = More foreign persuasin

Why is everyone talking about convict? How are they involved?

Ask foreman if I can just say "GUILTY" now so I can name it less time.

Try to find out what happened when I nodded off.

---

did I miss anything. Jury I could use a break?

Going to ignore all this 'forensic' palaver. Stuff and nonsense. Gut instinct far more valuable.

Been told off for laughing sarcastically when the criminal speaks. Can't I have an opinion?

Think judge is well aware of who I am. Taylor? possibly Soloway.

In my vast experience, it's always the person you suspect the least. Think

Judge might be in on this somehow.

Oh, it's a fraud thing. Thought it was murder. Sure someone mentioned murder. Maybe explains confused watch... of slaughter 'murderer' at criminal.

Can't decide when the best time to hand in... is... might be? ?

Blah Blah Blah. How can a non-weary Sunday Morning catalogue talk quite so much.

First divorced. I've been promising myself... how... for all these years.

Or his lawyer is? Yes it's probably him.

Oddy wants to talk to me — don't know why. Assume he wants something signed. Or promote me to Jeweller. Quite sensible.

Goodness these men do want a lot. Keep asking questions. From now on I'll be telling them to shut up.

Oh God, here comes a policeman. Can't stand policemen.

Not sure why this madness is enjoying? I was too busy giving current forensic duty today. Is she a prostitute? That hat suggests so.

As an expert, I have decided on halt proceedings and give my opinion of the case so far. Think I will help everyone. Judge has damn nerves early. Good. Possible cake I hope.

I have been dismissed. I'm assuming that having such a furious juror is a possible detriment. Or possibly the judge is once sort of freemason.

Never mind. The theatre of it all! Plus, lots of good stuff to see in books. How can judge say I'm in 'contempt of court'? I'm Agatha Christie! I love courts. The fools.

In my vast experience, it's always the person you suspect the least.
Think judge might be in on this somehow.

Oh, it's a fraud thing. Thought it was murder. Sure someone mentioned murder.
Might explain confused looks when I shouted 'murderer' at criminal.

Can't decide when the best time to hand out 'Mousetrap' flyers might be.

Blah, blah, blah. How can a man wearing such appalling cologne talk quite so much?

Just discovered I've been mispronouncing 'motive' incorrectly for all these years.
Or this lawyer is. Yes, it's probably him.

Judge wants to talk to me during the recess. Assume he wants something signed.
Or promote me to foreman. Quite sensible.

Goodness these men do shout a lot.
Getting quite hoarse from constantly telling them to shut up.

Oh God, here comes a policeman. Can't stand policemen.

Not sure why this witness is crying? I was too busy giving current foreman dirty looks.
Is she a prostitute? That hat suggests so.

As an expert, I have decided to halt proceedings and give my opinion of the case so far.
Think it will help everyone.

Judge has called recess early. Good. Possible cake I hope.

I have been dismissed. I'm assuming that having such a famous juror is a possible
distraction. Or possibly the judge is some sort of Freemason.

Will make the theatre after all! Plus, lots of good stuff to use in books. How can judge
say I'm in 'contempt of court'? I'm Agatha Christie! I love courts. The fools.

My dear Galileo,

Thank you so much for your letter extolling the virtues of your newly discovered telescope to such a passionate degree. Fourteen pages! Wow, you really love that telescope. I'm sure it's going to be really useful in your work as a scientist. As you know, I am just a poor carver, so it probably won't make that much of a difference to me. But glad to see it's going to give you so much joy.

Clara sends her love. Oh wait, sorry, no she doesn't. A fever took her this last winter. That's right, she's dead. Sorry you were too excited in your mammoth telescope letter to ask about her welfare. Or the welfare of anyone else for that matter. Like me, for instance, one of your oldest friends. Nothing. Not even a 'what's happening?'

Guess you're not too interested in my business, which is floundering, thanks for asking. Perhaps I could use your new, exciting telescope to view all my customers who have been stolen by Piereto down the street who slashed his prices and has unbelievably low overheads. Or I could use it to create some kind of makeshift gibbet or club to do away with myself now I am alone in the world apart from a yard full of rotting lumber and extensive, precise instructions on how to use a telescope from someone I thought was my friend.

Glad to hear that your pal the Doge is such a supporter of your new instrument and has rewarded you handsomely to utilise its development. The thought of you rolling around in all that new-found telescope money will surely keep me warm at night and also clothe and feed my children, who grow uglier by the day.

And me? How am I, a freshly minted widower with no assets and various offspring that resemble root vegetables? Well, now that I'm single and courting, I can impress dates with the cyst that has been growing on my neck. It's the size of an olive, if an olive was the size of a grapefruit. And it appears to have something inside it that moves. As well as impressing potential new mothers for my children, it's also a great way to drive the last remaining customers from my workshop in disgust. I run after them shouting, 'Come back! I have many telescopic facts to share with you!' But to no avail. Even the priest won't see me.

My dear Galileo,

Thank you so much for your letter extolling the virtues of your newly discovered telescope to such a passionate degree. Fourteen pages! Wow, you really love that telescope. I'm sure its going to be really usefull in your work as a scientist. As you know, I am just a poor curver, so it probably won't make that much of a difference to me. But glad to see its going to give you so much joy.

Clara sends her love. Oh wait, sorry, no she doesn't. A fever took her this last winter. That's right, she's dead. Sorry you were too excited in your mammoth telescope letter to ask about her welfare. Or the welfare of anyone else for that matter. Like me, for instance, one of your oldest friends. Nothing. Not even a whats happening?

Guess you're not too interested in my business, which is floundering, thanks for asking. Perhaps I could use your new exciting telescope to view all my customers who have been stolen by Piereto down the street who slashed his prices and has unbelievably low overheads. Or I could use it to create some kind of makeshift gibbet or club to do away with myself now I am alone in the world apart from a yard full of rotting timber. and extensive precise instructions on how to use a telescope from someone I thought was my friend.

Glad to hear that your pal the Doge is such a supporter of your new instrument and has rewarded you handsomely to utilise its development. The thought of you rolling around in all that new found telescope money will surely keep me warm at night and also clothe and feed my children. who grow uglier by the day

And me? How am I, a freshly minted widower with no assets and various offspring that resemble root vegetables? Well now that I'm single and courting I can impress dates with the cyst that had been growing on my neck. It's the size of an olive. If an olive was was the size of a grapefruit. And it appears to have something inside it that moves. As well as impressing potential new mothers for my children. its also a great way to drive the last remaining customers from my workshop in disgust. I run after them shouting. Come back! I have many telescopic facts to share with you! But to no avail. Even the priest wont see me.

Please do keep me up to date with any more fourteen-page developments of that tube you look through. Or, if it's too late, you can always pop along and read such information at my funeral. It should keep the congregation entertained in between eulogies describing my tragic, pitiful life. Why not bring a telescope along and show it off to everyone? 'Here, friends of the late Guisto, look at something I have achieved in my life, unlike that sad sack who is now dead in the ground. Alongside his wife who resembled a fat horse.'

I can't wait for the next thrilling instalment of 'The Telescope'. What will happen, I wonder? Perhaps you'll use it to look at something far away, or slightly closer, or right up your own arse.

I'll say goodbye now, for surely soon I'll be dead.
Guisto

P.S. Fuck you.

Please do keep me up to date with way more fourteen page developments of that tube you look through. Or, if its too late, you can always pop by and read such information at my funeral should keep the congregation entertained in between describing my tragic, pitiful life. Why not bring a telescope along and show it off to everyone? Here friends of the late Gusto, look at something I have achieved in my life unlike that sad sack who is now dead in the ground. Alongside his wife who resembled a fat horse.

I cant wait for the next thrilling instalment of The Telescope. What will happen i wonder? Perhaps youll use it to look at something far away, or slightly closer, or right up your own arse.

I'll say goodbye now for surely soon, I'll be dead.

Gusto

P.S. Fuck you

_____

14th January 1947

Mr Chowdry,

How can this possibly happen again?

I feel that this constant inability to handle my laundry requirements in an efficient manner is a deliberate act of provocation. I can see no other reason for your continued incompetence.

This latest blunder comes at the end of a long list of appalling aberrations. On opening my latest parcel from your establishment, I discovered clothing, which was beautifully washed, perfectly pressed and obviously not mine.

Inside I found some quite garish trousers in the tartan print of a clan unknown, some spats, a sort of lacy lady's bodice, a selection of ties and a chemise that an aide described to me as 'Hawaiian'.

Does that sound like me, Mr Chowdry? In our various and often heated meetings either here or on your premises have you ever seen me in tartan trousers or sock garters? I think you should have my personal style pretty much memorised by now. It tends to revolve around a similar theme.

Perhaps you remember the last time I used your services? On that occasion all of my dhotis were returned to me, coloured in a delightful shade of pink. And when I vigorously brought this to your attention, you claimed that one of my 'red socks' must have entered into the process in some way. As I expressed at the time, Mr Chowdry, please review any number of printed articles and newsreel footage, you will see that red socks have never been involved in my fashion routine.

And prior to this I sent you around eight dhotis to be cleaned, only for you to return one enormous one. I'm still baffled as to how you managed this. And before that there was the curious instance when my clothing was returned with crudely rendered images of food on them (pies and the like) and scrawled phrases such as 'yum yum' and 'food is delicious'. As this was during a well-publicised hunger strike, I can only assume this was either a poorly conceived joke or some act of political mischievousness.

With these continued laundry mishaps, Mr Chowdry, you are doing nothing to help the Quit India Movement. In fact you are personally hindering the cause and diverting energies required to sustain pressure on the British. I have endured much harassment, the curtailment of my liberty, swingeing character attacks and assassination attempts. But nothing gets my dander up to such a degree as your inability to wash a few dhotis. They're just dhotis! It's a big sheet. What's the problem here? Do you want me, a celebrated global figure, to go and launder the clothing myself? Perhaps on a big rock by the river? Yes, that is bound to impress world leaders when I'm in negotiations to further our cause. 'Hold on, Mr Roosevelt, I need to go and slap a sheet against a giant stone because Mr Chowdry can't get a simple dry cleaning order correct, even though that is his job.'

As you may be aware, prior to my efforts in assuring Indian independence I practised as a barrister and thus have a full understanding of my statutory rights. Rights that you have frequently abused, Mr Chowdry. Please don't turn this into a legal matter, sir, as you will surely lose. I also have many followers and supporters. They pay attention to me, Mr Chowdry. They have listened and reacted to my calls to stand up against our British oppressors. And, if at the end of a speech, I happened to slip in a 'by the way, don't bother to get your laundry done at Chowdry's, as you may find your own clothes have vanished only to be replaced by a large rabbit costume' (another incident I haven't forgotten), that could be very damaging.

Furthermore, I'm sure that you know that I am a proponent of non-violent protest. However, in your case I am willing to make an exception and I feel we are reaching the point where my only recourse will be the insertion of a sandal somewhere upon your person.

~~Sincerely~~ Angrily,
Gandhi

14th January 1947

Mr Chandry,

How can this possibly happen again?

I feel that this inability to handle my laundry requirements in an efficient manner is a deliberate act of provocation. I can see no other reason for your continued incompetence.

The latest blunder comes at the end of a long list of appalling aberrations. On opening my latest parcel from your establishment, I discovered clothing which was beautifully washed, perfectly pressed and decidedly not mine.

Inside I found some quite garish trousers in a tartan print of a clan unknown, some spats, a sort of lacy lady's bodice, a selection of ties and a chemise that in colour

disclosed to me as "Tasmania".
Does that sound like me, Mr Clardy?
In air various and often heated
meetings either here or on your
premises have you ever seen me
in tartan trousers or such gaiters?

I think you should have my
personal style pretty much memorised
by now. It tends to revolve
around a similar theme.

Perhaps you remember the first
time I used your services? At that
occasion all of my theories were relevant
to me, and a delightful
dude it puts. And when I
rigorously brought this to your
collection, you claimed that one
of my 'red socks' must have
entered into the process in
some way. As I expressed at the
time, Mr Clardy, please review
any number of printed articles
and reviewed footage, you will see
that red socks have never been

involved in my public routine. And prior to this I sent you around eight photos to be signed, only for you to return one enormous one. I'm still baffled as to how you managed this. And before that there was the curious instance when my clothing was returned ~~to these~~ with crudely rendered images of food on them (pies and the like) and scrawled phrases such as 'yum yum' and 'food is delicious'. As this was during a well-publicised hunger strike, I can only assume this was either a poorly conceived joke or some act of political misdemeanors.

With these continued laundry mishaps, Mr Chaudry, you are doing nothing to help the Quit India Movement. In fact you are personally hindering the cause and diverting energies required to sustain pressure on the British. I have enclosed such harassment, the curtailment of my liberty, swinging character attacks and assassination attempts. But nothing gets my dander up to such a degree as your unability to smash a few dishes. They're just dishes! It's no big deal. What's the problem here? Do you want me, a celebrated global figure, to go and launder the clothing myself? Perhaps on a big pole by a river? Yes, that is bound to impress world leaders when I'm in negotiations to further our cause. Hold on Mr Roosevelt I need to go and bag a sheet against a giant stone because Mr Gandhi can't get a simple day's cleaning order correct, even though their is his job!

As you may be aware, prior to my efforts in winning Indian independence, I practiced as a barrister and thus have a full understanding of my statutory rights. Rights that you have frequently abused, Mr Charsly. Please don't turn this into a legal matter sir, as you will surely see. I also have many followers and congregations. They pay attention to me, Mr Chowdry. They have listened and reacted to my calls to stand up against our British oppressors. And, if at ~~the~~ the end of the speech, I happened to slip in a 'By the way, don't bother to get your laundry done at Chowdry's ~~as~~ as you may find your own clothes have vanished only to be replaced by a large rabbit costume' (another incident I haven't forgotten), that could be very damaging.

Furthermore, I'm sure that you know that I am a proponent of non-violent protest. However, in your case I am willing to make an exception and I feel we are reaching the point where my only recourse will be the insertion ~~of~~ of a sandal somewhere upon your person.

~~Sincerely Angrily~~

MK Gandhi

Johnny,

Thanks for your thoughts. Sorry to bitch and moan to you like that, just feeling a little under-exposed lately. I want Bo Diddley to be the biggest act in the world, that's all. I know you want that too.

I love some of your suggestions on how to make this happen and increase my exposure. Certainly some kind of collaboration makes sense and I'm intrigued by the idea of an album of cover versions.

But Johnny, really, changing my name? Are you crazy? I appreciate you think I might be taken more seriously as an artist if I wasn't called Diddley, but I think the ship may have sailed on that one.

Can I point out the fact that 147 of my 156 current recorded numbers have the words 'Bo' or 'Diddley' in there somewhere, as have the titles of all my albums.

For instance there's Bo Diddley, Hey Bo Diddley, Ho Bo Diddley, Hey Ho Bo Diddley, Sleigh Bo Diddley (from my Christmas album, Christmas Bo Diddley), Bo Bo Diddley, Go Bo Diddley, Stop Bo Diddley, Run Bo Diddley, Bo Diddley is a Gunslinger, Bo Diddley is a Weather Man, Bo Diddley is a Bo Diddley, Bo Diddley is a Guitar Player, There is Only One Bo Diddley, Here's Another Bo Diddley, Bo Diddley's Bo Diddley.

JOHNNY

THANKS FOR YOUR THOUGTS. SORRY TO BITCH AND
MOAN LIKE THAT, JUST FEELING A LITTLE UNDER-
EXPOSED LATELY. I WANT BO DIDDLEY TO BE THE
BIGGEST ACT IN THE WORLD, THATS ALL. I KNOW
YOU WANT THAT TOO.

I LOVE SOME OF YOUR SUGGESTIONS ON HOW TO
MAKE THIS HAPPEN AND INCREASE MY EXPOSURE.
CERTAINLY SOME KIND OF COLLABORATION
MAKES SENSE AND I'M INTRIGUED BY THE IDEA
OF AN ALBUM OF COVER VERSIONS.

BUT JOHNNY, REALLY. CHANGING MY NAME?
ARE YOU CRAZY? I APPRECIATE YOU THINK I
MIGHT BE TAKEN MORE SERIOUSLY AS AN
ARTIST IF I WASN'T CALLED DIDDLEY, BUT I
THINK THE SHIP MAY HAVE SAILED ON THAT
ONE.

CAN I POINT OUT THAT 147 OF MY 156 CURRENT
RECORDED NUMBERS HAVE THE WORDS 'BO' OR
'DIDDLEY' IN THERE SOMEWHERE, AS HAVE THE
TITLES OF ALL MY ALBUMS.

FOR INSTANCE THERE'S BO DIDDLEY, HEY BO DIDDLEY,
HO BO DIDDLEY, HEY HO BO DIDDLEY, SLEIGH BO
DIDDLEY (FROM MY CHRISTMAS ALBUM,
CHRISTMAS BO DIDDLEY), BO BO DIDDLEY,
GO BO DIDDLEY, STOP BO DIDDLEY, RUN BO

DIDDLEY, BO DIDDLEY IS A GUNSLINGER, BO DIDDLEY IS A WEATHER MAN, BO DIDDLEY IS A BO DIDDLEY, BO DIDDLEY IS A GUITAR PLAYER, THERE IS ONLY ONE BO DIDDLEY, HERES ANOTHER BO DIDDLEY, BO DIDDLEYS BO DIDDLEY.

THEN THERES BO DIDDLEYS LAMENT, BO AND THE DIDDLEYS, BO DIDDLEY AND COMPANY BO DIDDLEY ALONE, THE BO DIDDLEYS TRIO, BIG BAD BO DIDDLEY, SMALL NICE BO DIDDLEY, DIDDLEY DADDY, DON'T KNOW DIDDLEY, KNOW TOO MUCH DIDDLEY, STORY OF BO DIDDLEY, FURTHER TALES OF BO DIDDLEY, THE LAST STAND OF BO DIDDLEY, MORE OF THE LAST STAND OF BO DIDDLEY, BO DIDDLEYS BEAT, BO DIDDLEY RIDES AGAIN, BO DIDDLEY'S BEACH PARTY, BO DIDDLEY'S SKI PARTY, BO DIDDLEYS HANNUKA FAVOURITES.

AND OF COURS, BO DIDDLEY IN LONON, BO DIDDLEY IN ATHENS, BO DIDDLEY'S ATHENS

Then there's Bo Diddley's Lament, Bo and the Diddleys, Bo Diddley and Company, Bo Diddley Alone, The Bo Diddley Trio, Big Bad Bo Diddley, Small Nice Bo Diddley, Diddley Daddy, Don't Know Diddley, Know Too Much Diddley, Story of Bo Diddley, Further Tales of Bo Diddley, The Last Stand of Bo Diddley, More of the Last Stand of Bo Diddley, Bo Diddley's Beat, Bo Diddley Rides Again, Bo Diddley's Beach Party, Bo Diddley's Ski Party, Bo Diddley's Hannukah Favourites.

And of course, Bo Diddley in London, Bo Diddley in Athens, Bo Diddley's Athen's Beach Party, Bo's Bounce, Bo's Twist, Bo's Twist and Bounce, Diddley's Bounce, Diddley's Twist, Diddley's Bounce and Twist, Bo Diddley's Bounce, Bo Diddley's Twist, Bo Diddley's Bounce and Twist, Bo Diddley's Twist and Bounce and Do the Bo Diddley.

Change my name? Think Bo Diddley might need to change his publicist.

Yours, Bo Diddley

P.S. Bo Diddley

16th October 1902

Mishka,

You know I love doing business with you down at Botkin's Pets, you guys are the best in the biz. But listen, that last batch of dogs that you sent down here were just no use to me.

What you supplied, in scientific terms, is what's known as 'dry dogs'. I can't do anything with that, Mishka. Look, I know it sounds weird. 'Why would a man of science like Doctor Pavlov need any particular sort of dog?' Well, I can't really get into that, but dry dogs are useless to me.

I need real droolers, Mishka. Slobberers. The kind of animal that actually turns your stomach when they land their glistening, saliva-filled chops on your knee. A wet patch guaranteed every time.

Honestly (and again, I realise it sounds weird) the more spit-filled the better. If you look at the cur and say 'Jeez, I think there may be something medically wrong with this one, his face looks like a babbling brook', then you are on the right track. The last ones you sent over could barely form a puddle. It was like tumbleweeds coming out of these dogs. Real dry dogs.

Remember Doug? That Pit-bull you provided last summer? He was perfect. Dumb as a post and drooling all day long. With most of the animals here at the lab, we use a standard broom to clean out their cages. With Doug we actually had to use a mop and a number of squeegees. It was beautiful, Mishka. Though sadly, it turned out he was deaf, so no use to us at all.

Oh yeah, that's the other thing. No deaf ones, Mishka, they have to be able to hear. Again, I know that appears peculiar, but if you can just click your fingers or clap your hands, see if they turn their heads. They don't have to have perfect hearing or anything, as long as they can recognise basic ringing sounds and are nice and slobbery.

Again, no point in going into why I need all this, it has to do with experiments. But Mishka, we need good, moist dogs who have basic hearing potential. Really, nothing else matters. Size, colour, number of limbs – that doesn't concern me. Just make sure they drool and hear and we can continue doing business.

Yours in anticipation,
Dr Ivan Pavlov

3rd March 1949

Dear George,

Thank you so much for sending me the manuscript of the new book. I thoroughly enjoyed it and thought it had some jolly shocking moments. Your vision of a futuristic world four decades hence is certainly a chilling one. Real food for thought. I did have a few questions, however, which I've outlined below.

1. You refer frequently to the 'warmers of the leg' that many of the ladies in your futuristic dystopia choose to wear, especially during exercise. Is there some environmental condition in the future that brings out this climatic discomfort in that particular part of the body? And while the rest of the world you so vividly portray is drab and grim, these 'warmers' are often in vibrant, almost fluorescent hues. It seems a little out of place. I have similar qualms about the 'colourful bands of the head' they also wear on occasion.

2. I think the idea of the populous communicating via portable telephones is very novel, if slightly farfetched. But I do wonder, if they have the technology to create these magical devices, why make them so big? You describe them as 'the size of a brick, with a stout, rigid aerial at the outer edge'. This seems rather impractical. If they are indeed portable, I don't quite understand why they can't fit into the palm of the hand.

3. The twist at the end where Big Brother is revealed to be not only a woman but a woman of modest means from Lincolnshire, struck me as tonally confusing. Even in this horrifying world, I can't really picture a woman from this economic stratum rising to the role of supreme leader and wielding such influence on a nation. And while I understand your personal beliefs in regards to the working man, her irrational hatred of miners feels like a diversion. Might it be better to keep it vague?

Dear George,

Thank you so much for sending me the manuscript of the new book. I thoroughly enjoyed it and thought it had some jolly shocking moments. Your vision of a futuristic world four decades hence is certainly a chilling one. Real food for thought. I did have a few questions, however, which I've outlined below.

1. You refer frequently to the 'warmers of the leg' that many of the ladies in your futuristic dystopia choose to wear, especially during exercise. Is there some environmental condition in the future that brings out this climatic discomfort in that particular part of the body? And while the rest of the world you so vividly portray is drab and grim, these 'warmers' are often in vibrant, almost fluorescent hues. It seems a little out of place. I have similar qualms about the 'colourful bands of the head' they also wear on occasion.

2. I think the idea of the populous communicating via portable telephones is very novel, if slightly farfetched. But I do wonder, if they have the technology to create these magical devices, why make them so big? You describe them as 'the size of a brick, with a stout, rigid aerial at the outer edge'. This seems rather impractical. If they are indeed portable, I don't quite understand why they can't fit into the palm of the hand.

3. The twist at the end where Big Brother is revealed to be not only a woman but a woman of modest means from Lincolnshire, struck me as tonally confusing. Even in this horrifying world, I can't really picture a woman from this economic stratum rising to the role of supreme leader and wielding such influence on a nation. And while I understand your personal beliefs in regards to the working man, her irrational hatred of miners feels like a diversion. Might it be better to keep it vague?

4. I didn't really understand the section describing the 'small rotating cube, highlighted with colours, that transfixed all of Oceania who would spend hours besotted by its puzzlement'. I'm afraid I can't really picture that at all. Even with the four-page instructional guide explaining how to defeat this brainteaser with a series of diagrams and tips on where to put various fingers to ensure success. It rather took me away from the story.

5. While naming the character of Winston's chief torturer as 'Russ Abbot' is fine, calling the place where the torture occurs as his 'Madhouse' struck an odd note with me. With the character enduring such harrowing occurrences there, the current name has a dash of light entertainment about it. And the subsequent chapter about Mr Abbot's singing career seemed frivolous, despite the atmosphere you created.

6. The legion of wealthy young sociopaths who are powered by a white powder while wearing braces and spectacles featuring vibrantly coloured frames may be too obnoxious to include, even in the grim world of 1984.

7. I think the idea of the counter-revolutionary group being called The Brotherhood is acceptable, but don't really like it being shortened to Bros. Loses its power somehow.

8. Also, the long section about The Brotherhood obtaining funds thanks to the virtues of a 'foul-mouthed Irishman, with long unkempt hair and aggressive tendencies' releasing a 78rpm recording that would be 'heard every year, when the birth of Christ is celebrated' was confusing. But I'd keep in the bit with the rats.

9. The 'Anti-Sex League' may get us into trouble with the Royal Chamberlain, but I think it should stay. However, I think the 'Just Say No' campaign that Julia instigates might be overkill, especially when she emblazons her clothing with orders to 'Relax' and the like. I would imagine that the 'Thought Police' that you describe so well would soon put pay to all that.

Despite these few qualms, I think what we have here is a cracking read and with these few amendments I have no doubt it will be your most successful work to date.

            Yours sincerely,

                        Finbar
                        Secker & Warburg Publishers
                        London

P.S. Mr Disney has been back in touch about turning the talking pig book into an animated musical. I trust you have no objections to this?

4. I didn't really understand the section describing the 'small rotating cube, highlighted with colours, that transfixed all of Oceania who would spend hours besotted by its puzzlement'. I'm afraid I can't really picture that at all. Even with the four-page instructional guide explaining how to defeat this brainteaser with a series of diagrams and tips on where to put various fingers to ensure success. It rather took me away from the story.

5. While naming the character of Winston's chief torturer as 'Russ Abbot' is fine, calling the place where the torture occurs as his 'Madhouse' struck an odd note with me. With the character enduring such harrowing occurrences there, the current name has a dash of light entertainment about it. And the subsequent chapter about Mr Abbot's singing career seemed frivolous, despite the atmosphere you created.

6. The legion of wealthy young sociopaths who are powered by a white powder while wearing braces and spectacles featuring vibrantly coloured frames may be too obnoxious to include, even in the grim world of 1984.

7. I think the idea of the counter-revolutionary group being called The Brotherhood is acceptable, but don't really like it being shortened to Bros. Loses its power somehow.

8. Also, the long section about The Brotherhood obtaining funds thanks to the virtues of a 'foul-mouthed Irishman, with long unkempt hair and aggressive tendencies' releasing a 78rpm recording that would be 'heard every year, when the birth of Christ is celebrated' was confusing. But I'd keep in the bit with the rats.

9. The 'Anti-Sex League' may get us into trouble with the Royal Chamberlain, but I think it should stay. However, I think the 'Just Say No' campaign that Julia instigates might be overkill, especially when she emblazons her clothing with orders to 'Relax' and the like. I would imagine that the 'Thought Police' that you describe so well would soon put pay to all that.

Despite these few qualms, I think what we have here is a cracking read and with these few amendments I have no doubt it will be your most successful work to date.

Yours sincerely,

Finbar
Secker & Warburg Publishers
London

P.S. Mr Disney has been back in touch about turning the talking pig book into an animated musical. I trust you have no objections to this?

Happy Father's Day
That's a bloody joke
A father's day is perpetually black and dark and black
Perhaps further's day makes more sense
As you're further away from being human than you were previously.

Get well soon
You won't though will you
It will choke you from the inside
Like a rat squeaking, stuck up a bloody drainpipe
That's too small for it.

Season's Greetings
Christ.
The seasons greet you with complete indifference
They greet you cold and wet and black
Pump you full of shit in all directions
That you all wrap up and spill out
Under a stupid dying tree
In front of some terrible wallpaper.

Congratulations on the birth of your child
Yes, good luck with that one
They'll have the shit kicked out of them
Then they'll turn around and bite you in the face
Friendly fire they called it
Only it wasn't very friendly at all
Was it?

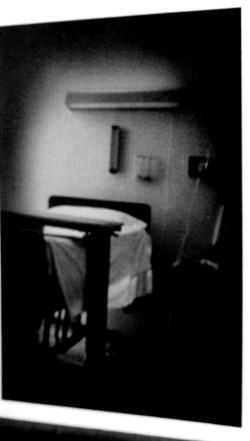

Valentine's Day,
I'd rather have my arse blown off,
And my guts exploded,
Through my eyes and mouth.
Why don't you just stick it up your arse?
And up your girlfriend's arse,
While you're at it?

Valentine's Day

I'd rather have my arse blown off.
And my guts exploded,
Through my eyes and mouth.
Why don't you just stick it up your arse?
And up your girlfriend's arse,
While you're at it?

21 today

I would say it was all downhill from here,
But that would be a lie.
It's all bloody uphill,
And there are big bloody spikes on the hill,
And dirt and grit and gravel,
And shit that gets in the big wounds
That the spikes have made.
You've got the key to the door.
But behind the door is a room
Filled with blades and piss-stained buggers.

They turned all the lights off
And had a blind man do the rewiring
You couldn't see a bloody hand before your face
Which was lucky as it wasn't your hand
And it wore a black glove and was in a bag
And was so close to your face you could feel the talons
Against your skin.
Happy Ruby Wedding Anniversary

BEATRIX POTTER TRIES TO GET AN OVERDRAFT EXTENSION

3rd April 1912

Oh Mr Clayton,

This little bunny has been ever so silly …

She just scampered over to the carrot patch but then found out that all of her carrots have gone …

The rabbits need carrots to grow big and strong and also to settle a recent unexpected income tax request. So this clever little bunny asked her good handsome friend at the bank, Mr Clayton, to give her a few more carrots just until the end of the month, when a cheque is expected …

If he could do this, until the 24th at the very latest, then it would make all the bunnies that live in Peppermint Farm ever so merry …

But if he is a big meanie and can't help the little bunnies get any more carrots, then who knows what may happen in the dell …

Yours hopefully,
Beatrix Potter

P.S. If it isn't clear, the bunny is me and the carrots are money.

Apr 3rd

Oh Mr Clayton .

This little bunny has been
ever so silly...

She just scampered over to
the carrot patch but then found
out that all of her carrots have gone...

The rabbits need
carrots to grow big
and strong
and also to
settle a recent
unexpected income tax request.

So this clever little bunny asked her good handsome friend at the bank, Mr Clayton, to give her a few more carrots just until the end of the month, when a cheque is expected...

If he could do this, until the 24th at the very latest, then it would make all the bunnies that live in Peppermint Farm ever so merry...

But if he is a big meanie and can't
help the little bunnies get any more
carrots, then who knows what may
happen in the dell...

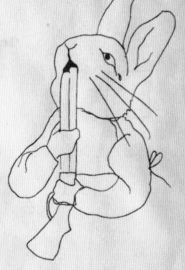

Yours hopefully,
Beatrix Potter

P.S. If it isn't clear, the bunny
is me and the carrots are money.

ACKNOWLEDGEMENTS!

Profound thanks to Lucy Peden for all her inspiration, Madeleine Brettingham for all her help, James Brown and all at Sabotage Times (where some of these letters first appeared).

Shawn Usher and
Letters of Note
for their understanding,
Scott and Rachel at
the Friday Project
and We Are Lauren for
their design expertise.

We Are Laura
The Rose Lipman Building
43 De Beauvior Rd
London
N1 5SQ

We hope you have enjoyed reading this book as much as we enjoyed designing it.

Thanks to Naomi Ashworth for her marvellous design assistance and to Dale and The Friday Project for giving us the dream job.

We Are Laura is a creative design studio that was founded in east London by Middlehurst and Woolf. (Can you guess our first names?) We specialise in bringing unique creative projects to life through design and installation.

To find out more about what we do, please visit:
www.wearelaura.co.uk

(Shameless self-promotion)

WE ARE LAURA

@We_are_Laura